MW00667261

RECORDED VERSIONS GUITAR

AUTHENTIC TRANSCRIPTIONS WITH NOTES AND TABLATURE

CAGE THE ELEP

THANK YOU HAPPY BIRTHDAY

Music transcriptions by Pete Billmann and Addi Booth

ISBN 978-1-4584-0123-6

HAL•LEONARD® CORPORATION

7777 W. BLUEMOUND RD. P.O. BOX 13819 MILWAUKEE, WI 53213

For all works contained herein:
Unauthorized copying, arranging, adapting, recording, Internet posting, public performance, or other distribution of the printed music in this publication is an infringement of copyright.
Infringers are liable under the law.

Visit Hal Leonard Online at
www.halleonard.com

Always Something

Words and Music by Brad Shultz, Daniel Tichenor, Jared Champion, Lincoln Parish and Matt Shultz

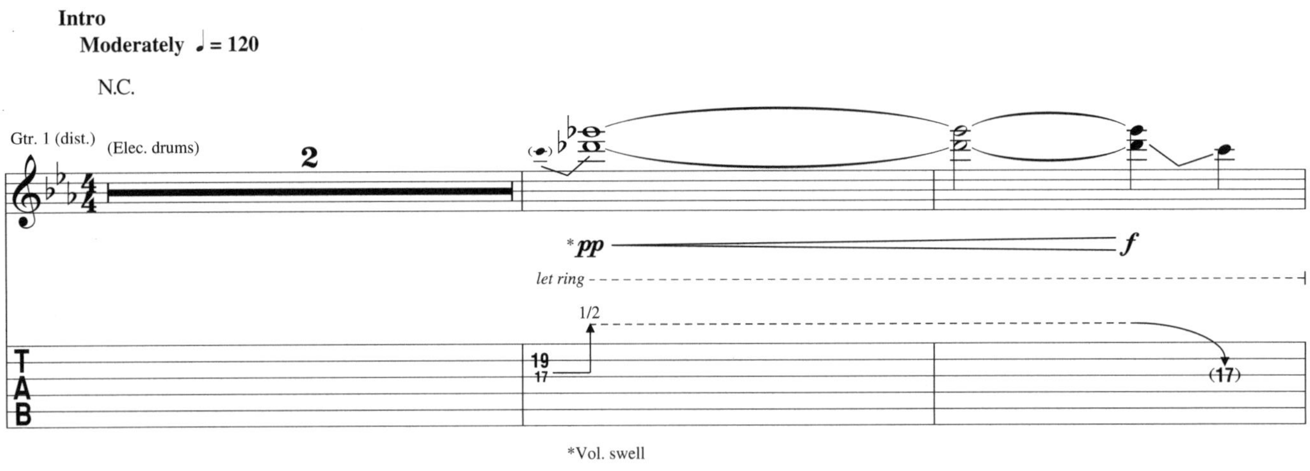

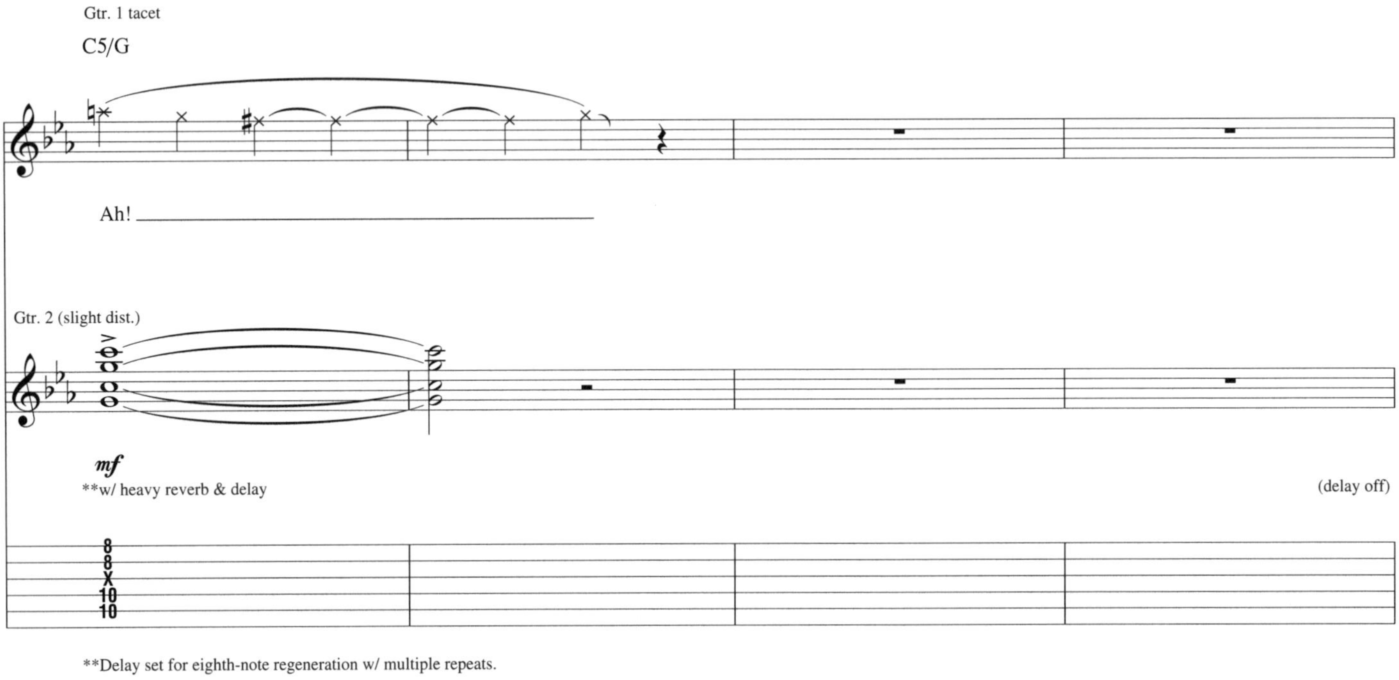

Copyright © 2010 Sony/ATV Music Publishing LLC, R And R Nomad Music Publishing Co. and 4U2ASKY Entertainment Inc.
All Rights on behalf of Sony/ATV Music Publishing LLC and R And R Nomad Publishing Co.
Administered by Sony/ATV Music Publishing LLC, 8 Music Square West, Nashville, TN 37203
International Copyright Secured All Rights Reserved

Gtr. 2 tacet
*Cm
Rhy. Fig. 1A
End Rhy. Fig. 1A
Gtr. 4 (clean)
mp
**w/ octaver
**Set for one octave above w/ effect signal only audible.
Rhy. Fig. 1
End Rhy. Fig. 1
Gtr. 1
mf
Gtr. 3 (clean)
mp
w/ amp tremolo
*Chord symbols reflect overall harmony.
Gtrs. 1 & 4: w/ Rhy. Figs. 1 & 1A
Gtr. 3
w/ bar
Verse
Gtr. 1: w/ Rhy. Fig. 1 (2 times)
1st time, Gtr. 4: w/ Rhy. Fig. 1A
2nd time, Gtr. 4: w/ Rhy. Fig. 1A (1 1/2 times)
Cm
1. Ear - ly in the morn-ing, rise to meet the sun. Work so hard to feed your wife, no time to show her lov - in'. In the
2. On your way back home a - gain, _ a good sa-mar - i - tan, _ you see a man _ stuck in the rain, _ strand-ed with _ no friends. And from the

*Two gtrs. arr. for one.

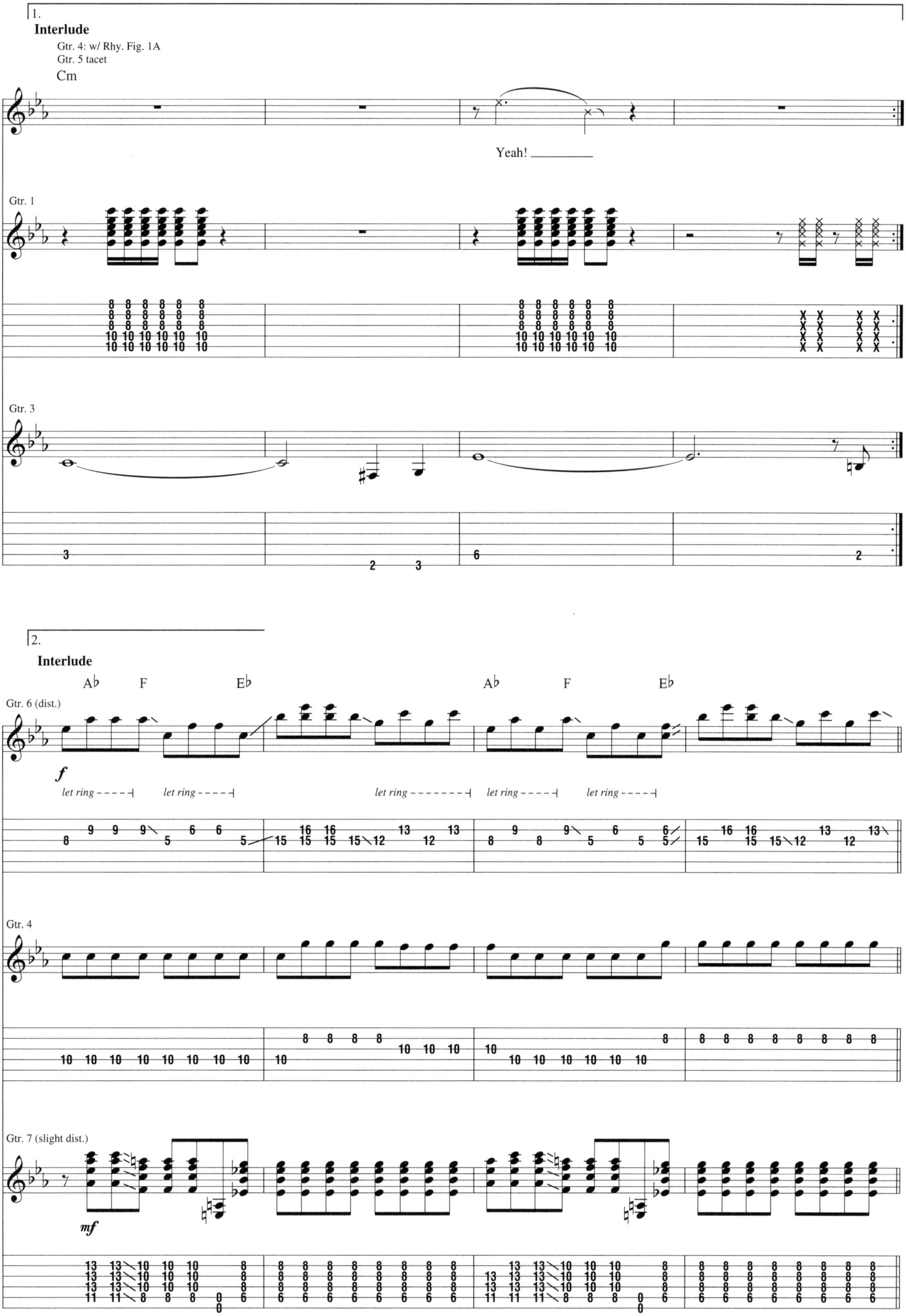
1.
Interlude
Gtr. 4: w/ Rhy. Fig. 1A
Gtr. 5 tacet
Cm
Yeah!
Gtr. 1
Gtr. 3
2.
Interlude
A♭
F
E♭
Gtr. 6 (dist.)
f
let ring
Gtr. 4
Gtr. 7 (slight dist.)
mf

Verse
Gtrs. 4 & 6 tacet
A♭ F E♭5 E♭ A♭ F5 E♭5 E♭
3. Mov-in' a-round, you nev - er see it com-ing. Burned by the light, you thought _ that you were run-ning.
Gtr. 7
A♭ F E♭ A♭ F E♭
Blind-ed a-gain, you're float - ing like a feath-er. Why can't you see you can't _ con-trol the weath-er?
Verse
Gtr. 7 tacet
N.C.
4. Some-times I caught my-self look-ing in the mir-ror with my eye - balls out and I'm look-ing at the fear. In the
Cm
bot-tom of the drain, saw it grow-ing like a plant. But it nev-er worked out the way I wrote it in my hands. I
Gtr. 4
Gtr. 1
*w/ delay
(delay off)
*Set for eighth-note regeneration w/ 10 repeats.

Gtr. 1 tacet
tried, I tried, I tried. De-cide, de - cide, de - cide, de - cide, de-cide, de -
D.S. al Coda
A♭ F E♭5 A♭ F E♭5
cide, de - cide, de - cide, de-cide, de - cide, de - cide, de - cide, de-cide, de...
(It's al - ways some - thing. It's al - ways some - thing.)
Gtr. 6
let ring
let ring
Gtr. 4
Gtr. 7

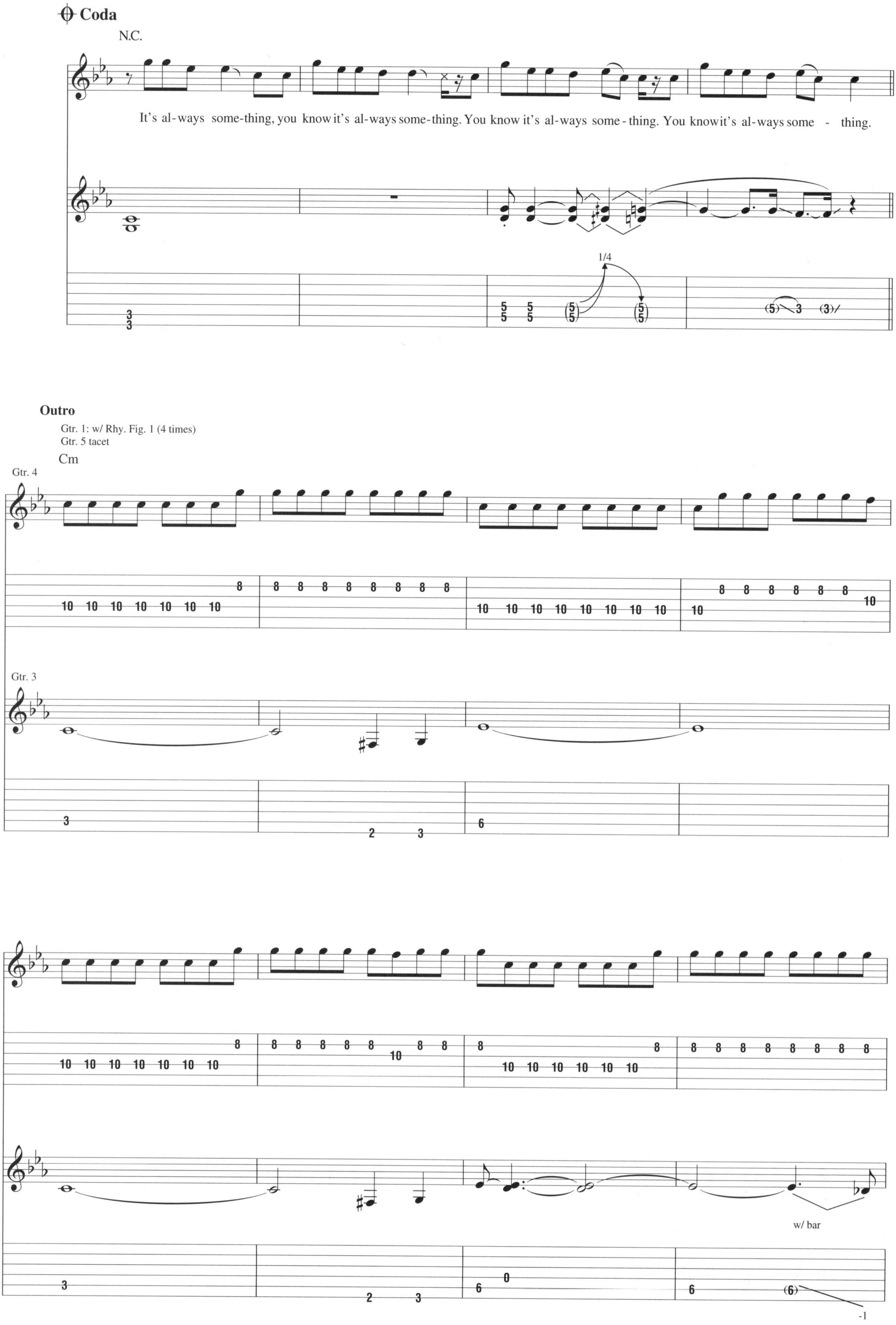
Coda
N.C.
It's al-ways some-thing, you know it's al-ways some-thing. You know it's al-ways some - thing. You knowit's al-ways some - thing.
1/4
Outro
Gtr. 1: w/ Rhy. Fig. 1 (4 times)
Gtr. 5 tacet
Cm
Gtr. 4
Gtr. 3
w/ bar
-1

Begin fade
let ring
w/ bar
Gtr. 3 tacet
Fade out
Gtr. 4
let ring
Gtr. 1

Aberdeen

Words and Music by Brad Shultz, Daniel Tichenor, Jared Champion, Lincoln Parish and Matt Shultz

Copyright © 2010 Sony/ATV Music Publishing LLC, R And R Nomad Music Publishing Co. and 4U2ASKY Entertainment Inc.
All Rights on behalf of Sony/ATV Music Publishing LLC and R And R Nomad Publishing Co.
Administered by Sony/ATV Music Publishing LLC, 8 Music Square West, Nashville, TN 37203
International Copyright Secured All Rights Reserved

Gtr. 2 tacet
*G5 E5 G5 E5 G5 E5 C5
Gtr. 2
p
Gtr. 1
8va
Harm.
**
*Chord symbols implied by bass, next 12 meas.
**Pluck strings behind bridge.
Verse
G5 E5 G5 E5 G5 E5
1. I've been try - ing real hard to, to re - al - ize,
Gtr. 1
8va
mf
fdbk.
Harm.
C5 G5 E5 G5 E5 G5 E5
but some things take a long, long, long, long time,
8va
Harm.
loco

G5 E5 C5 B5
long time.
Gtr. 2
15ma
f
*fdbk.
Pitch: A B A G
*Microphonic fdbk., not caused by string vibration.
Gtr. 1
f
Chorus
2nd time, Gtr. 3 tacet
G B Em C
Hold the phone, hit re - peat, got me foam - ing at the knees.
Riff B
loco
End Riff B
let ring
1/2
Rhy. Fig. 2
End Rhy. Fig. 2
Gtr. 1: w/ Rhy. Fig. 2 (2 times)
Gtr. 2: w/ Riff B (2 times)
G B Em C G B Em C
Saw the flame, tast-ed sin. You burned me once a - gain. Cut the cord, she's a creep. Ab - er - deen.

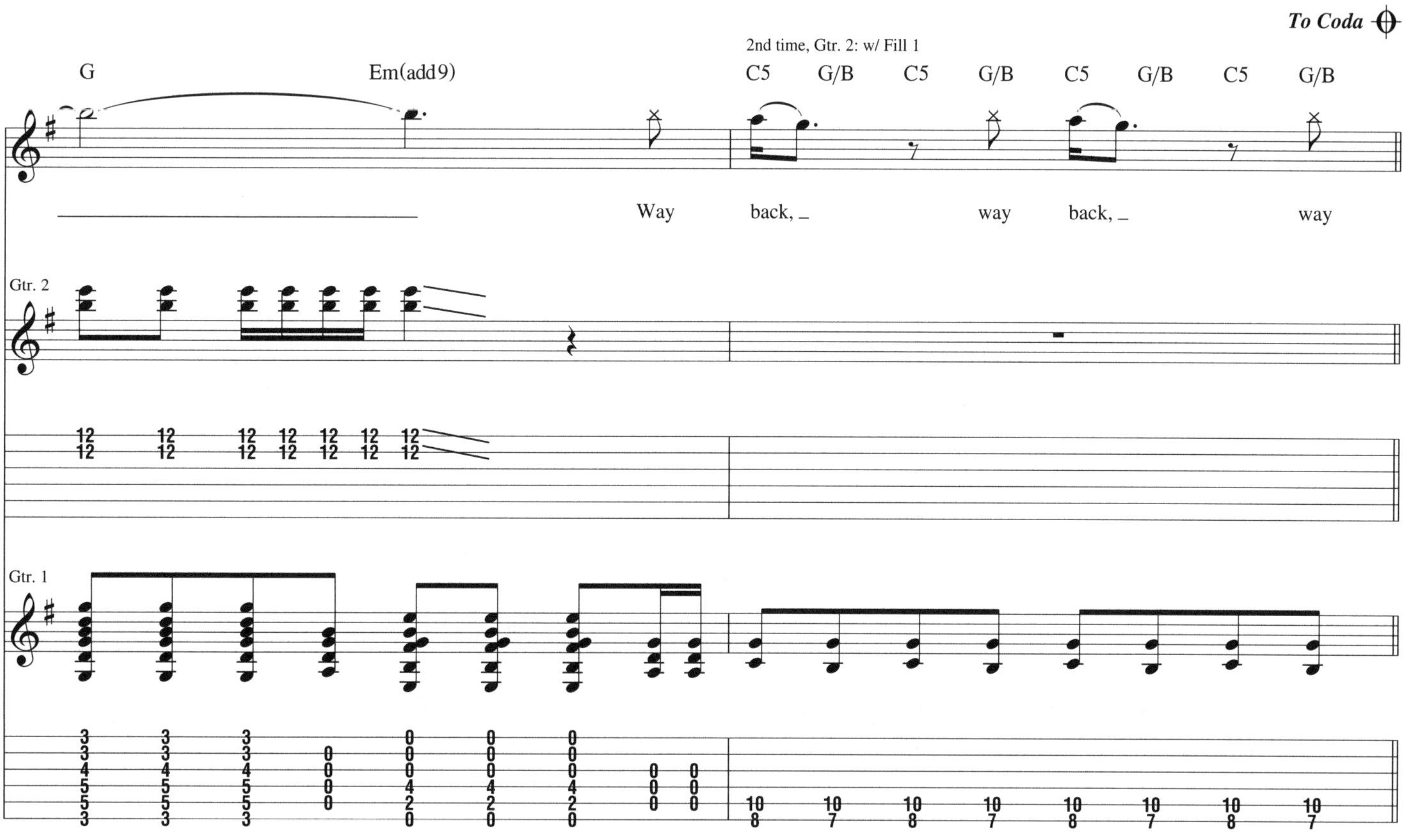

Interlude

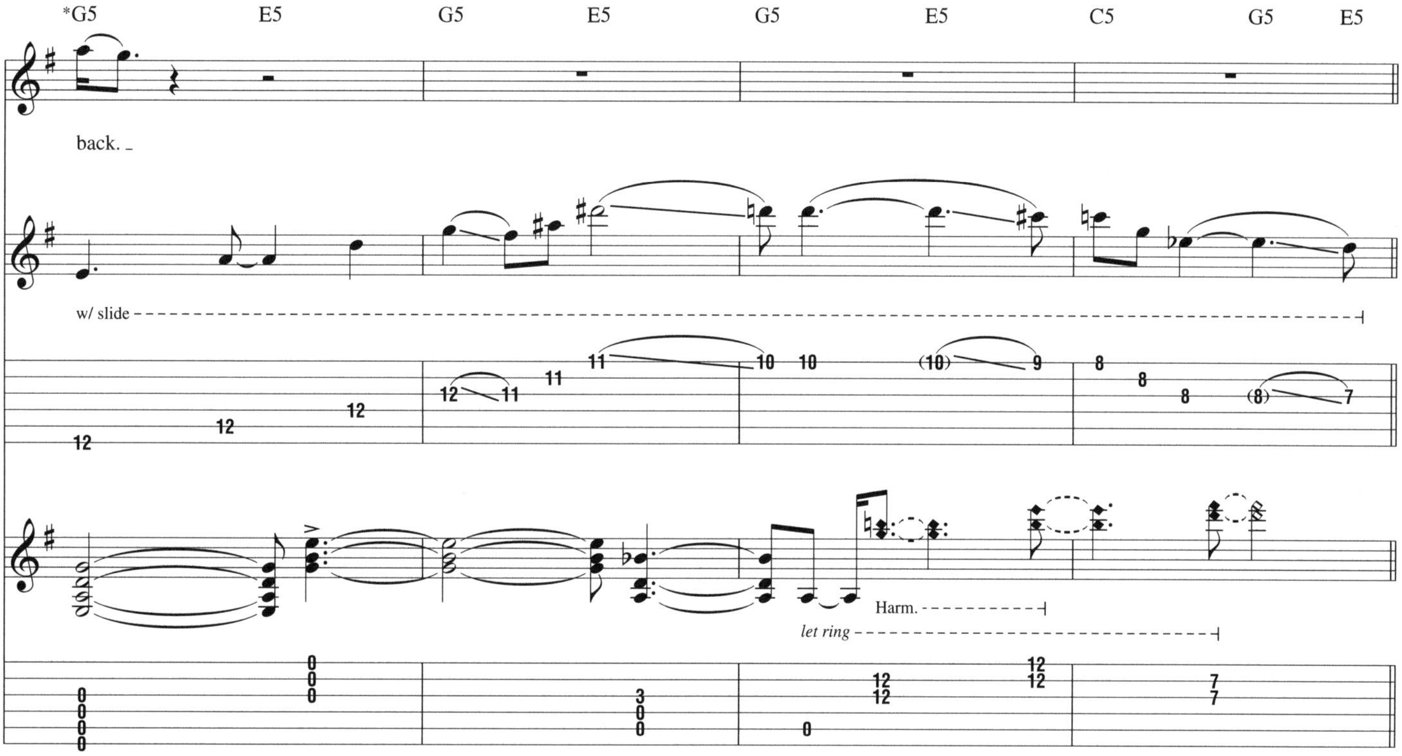

*Chord symbols implied by bass, next 12 meas.

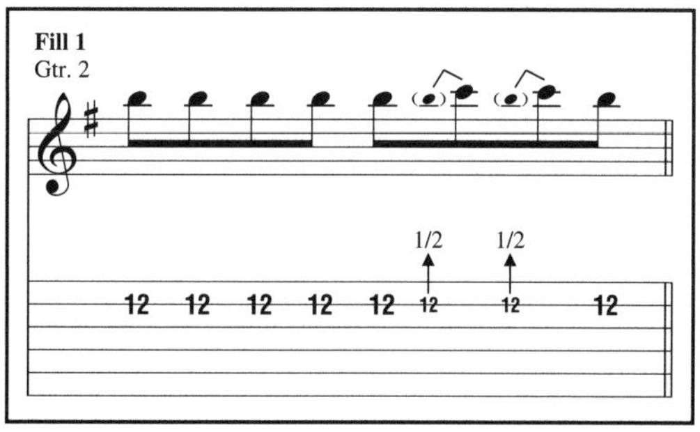

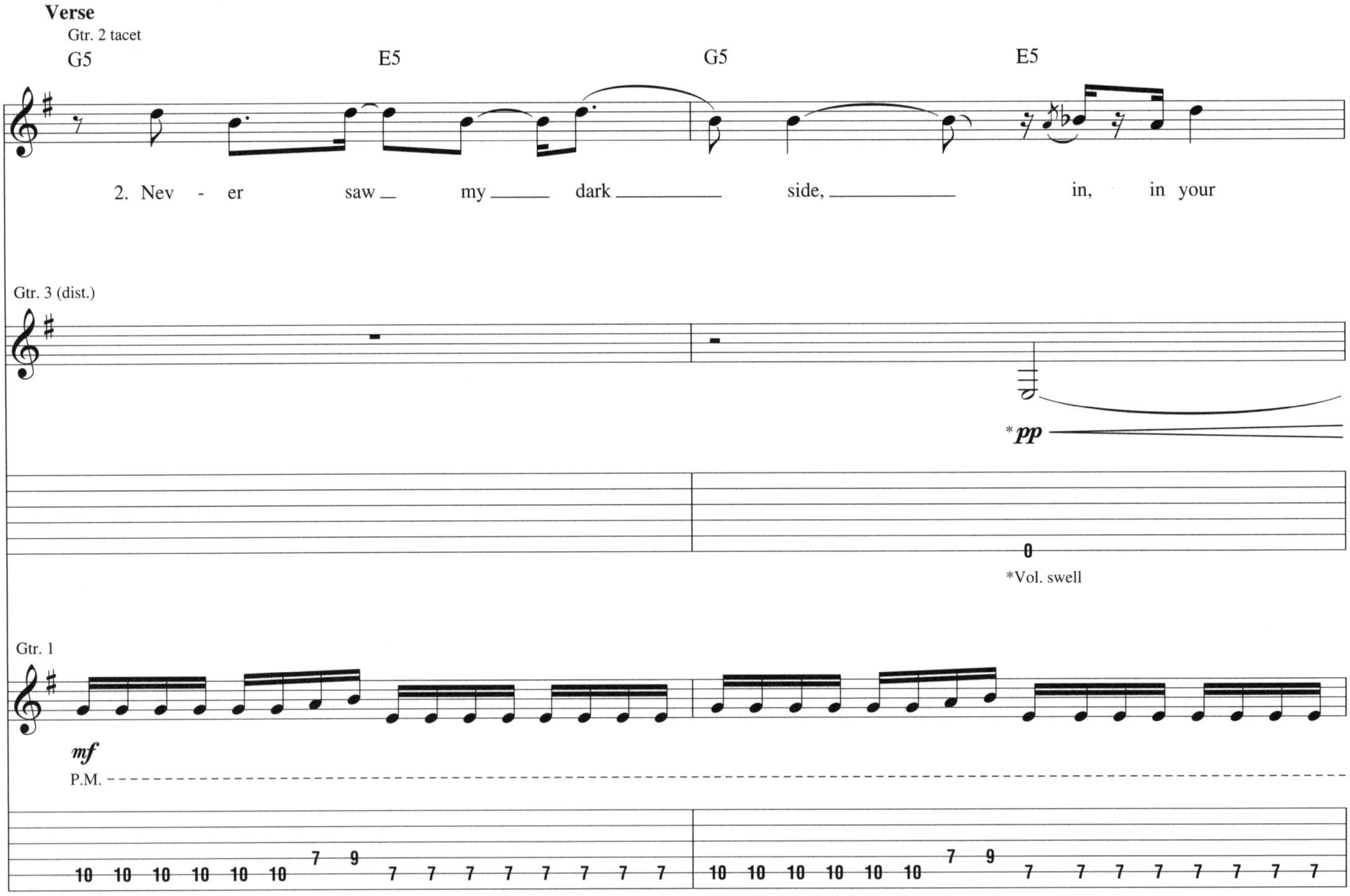
Verse
Gtr. 2 tacet
G5
E5
G5
E5
2. Nev - er saw my dark side, in, in your
Gtr. 3 (dist.)
*pp
*Vol. swell
Gtr. 1
mf
P.M.

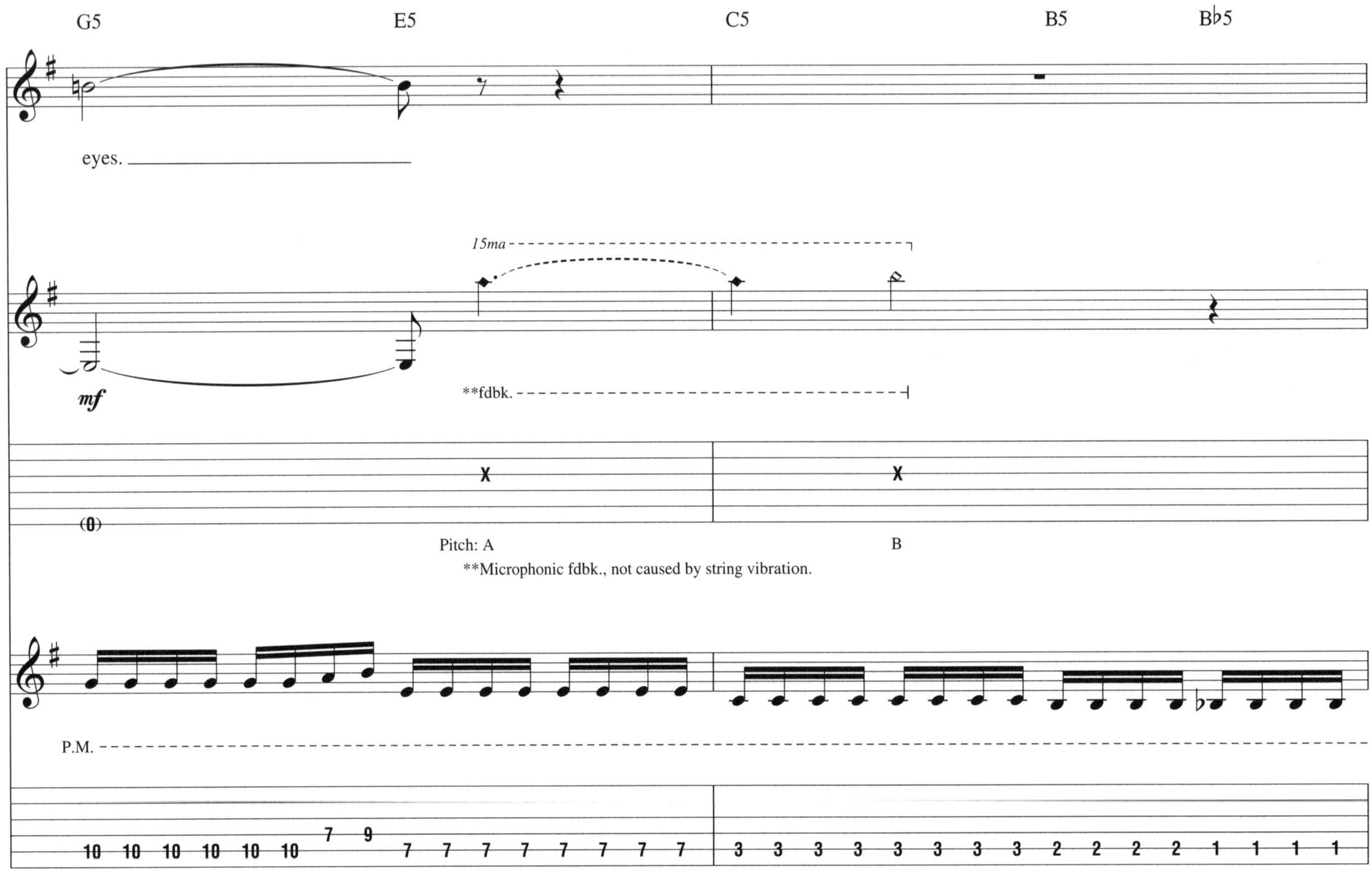
G5
E5
C5
B5
B♭5
eyes.
15ma
mf
**fdbk.
Pitch: A
B
**Microphonic fdbk., not caused by string vibration.
P.M.

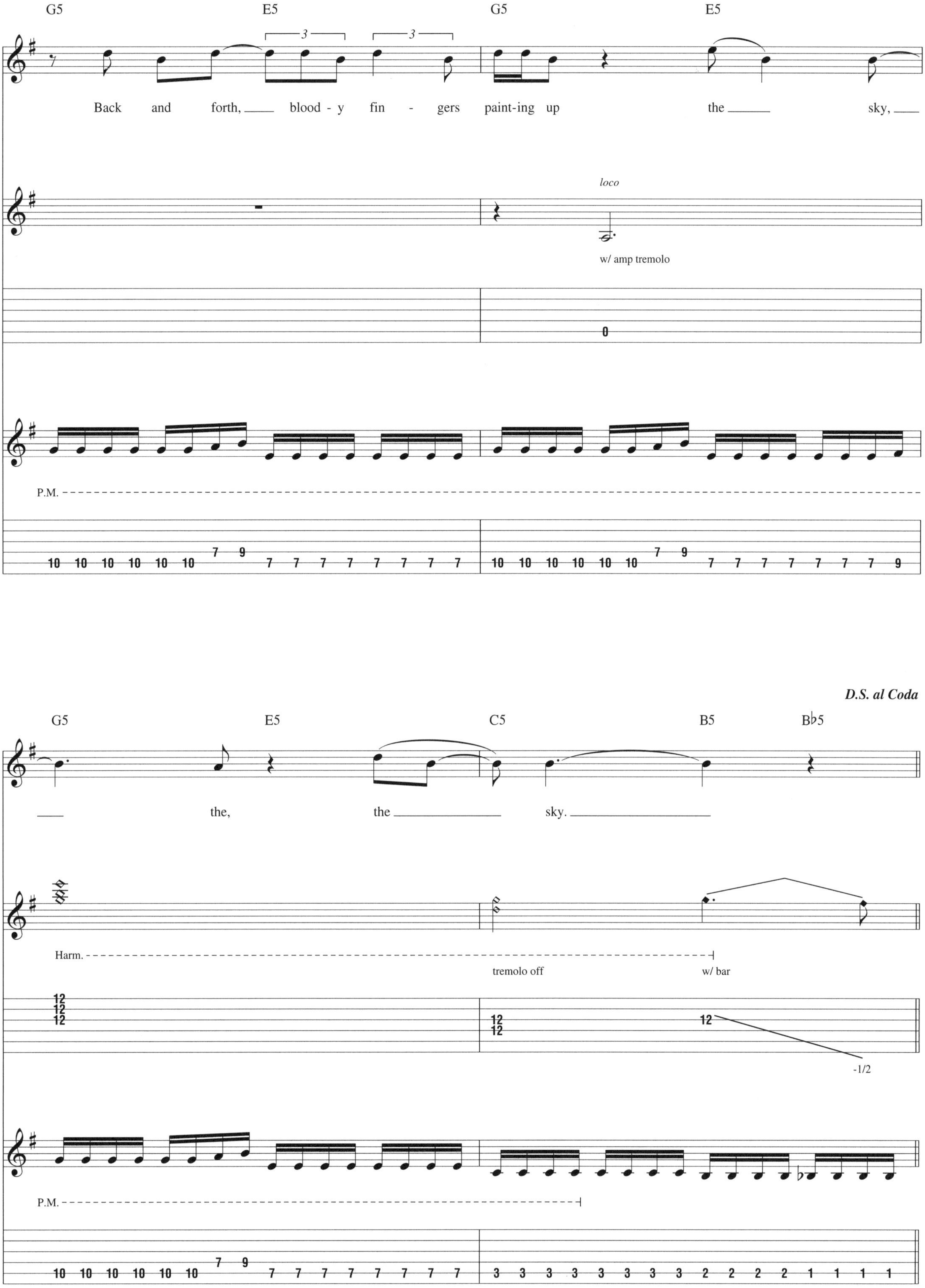
G5 E5 G5 E5
Back and forth, bloody - y fin - gers paint-ing up the sky,
loco
w/ amp tremolo
P.M.
D.S. al Coda
G5 E5 C5 B5 B♭5
the, the sky.
Harm.
tremolo off
w/ bar
-1/2
P.M.

Coda
Guitar Solo
E5
back!
Hey!
Hey!
*Gtrs. 2 & 3
*Composite arrangement
Gtr. 1
w/ amp tremolo
C5
B
Hey!
grad. bend
1/2
Interlude
Gtr. 1: w/ Rhy. Fig. 1 (2 times)
Gtr. 2: w/ Riff A
Gtr. 3 tacet
G5
B5
C
G5
B5
C
Oo, ___
oo, ___
ah.

*Refers to downstemmed vocs. only.

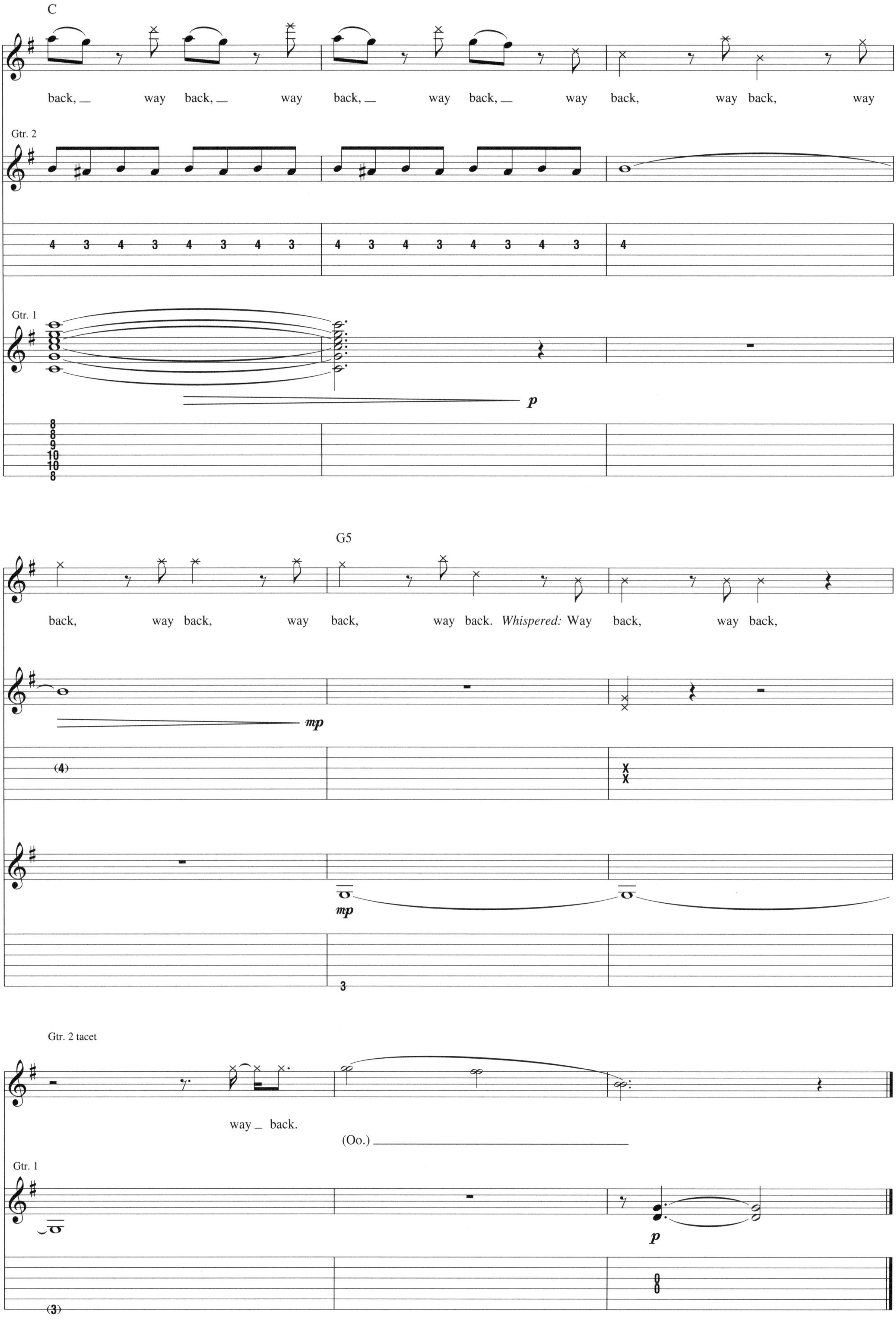
C
back, __ way back, __ way back, __ way back, __ way back, way back, way
Gtr. 2
Gtr. 1
p
G5
back, way back, way back, way back. Whispered: Way back, way back,
mp
mp
Gtr. 2 tacet
way _ back.
(Oo.)
Gtr. 1
p

Indy Kidz

Words and Music by Brad Shultz, Daniel Tichenor, Jared Champion, Lincoln Parish and Matt Shultz

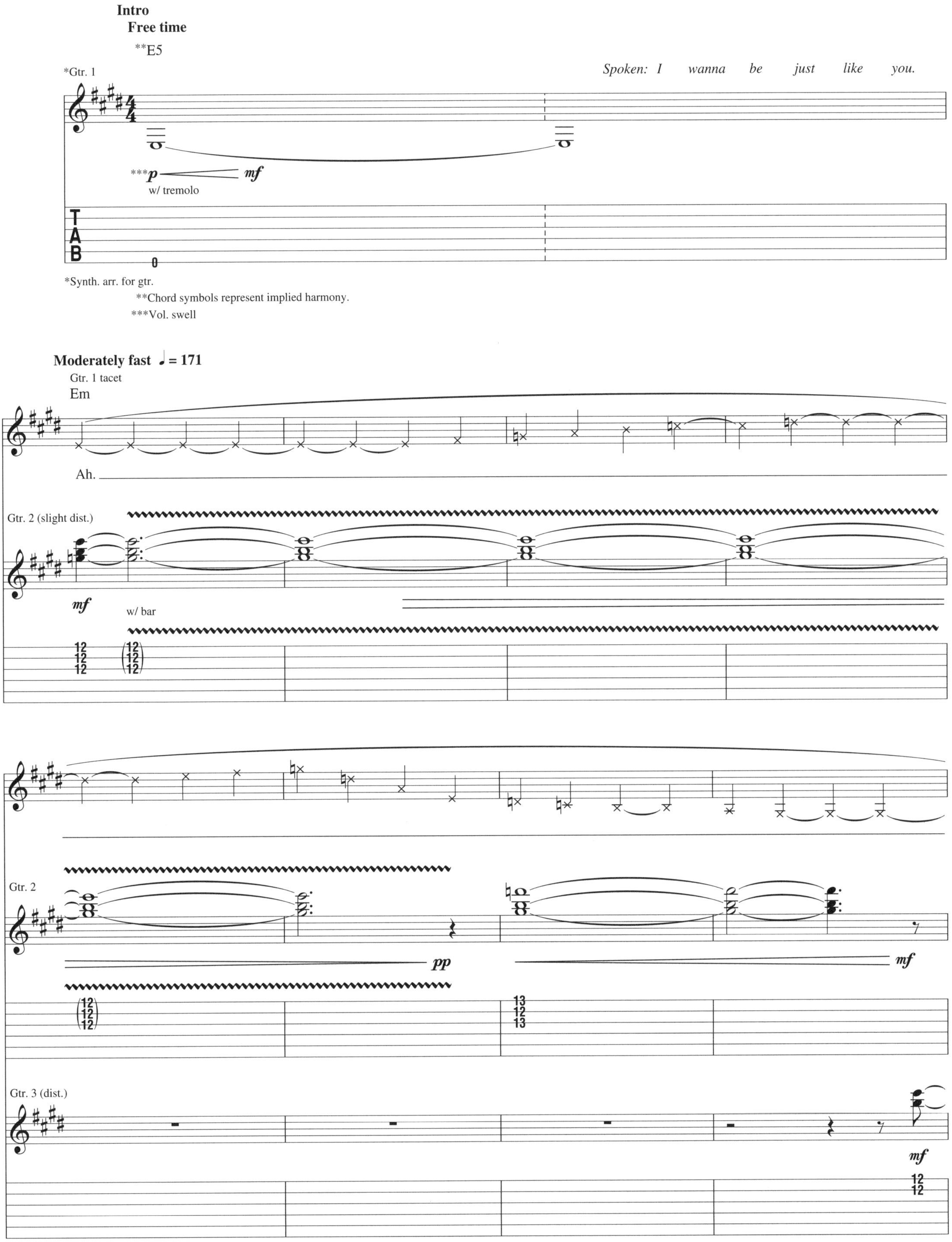

Copyright © 2010 Sony/ATV Music Publishing LLC, R And R Nomad Music Publishing Co. and 4U2ASKY Entertainment Inc.
All Rights on behalf of Sony/ATV Music Publishing LLC and R And R Nomad Publishing Co.
Administered by Sony/ATV Music Publishing LLC, 8 Music Square West, Nashville, TN 37203
International Copyright Secured All Rights Reserved

Gtr. 2 tacet
Gtr. 3
fdbk.
Pitch: C
Gtr. 3 tacet
Yeah! Yeah! Yeah! Yeah! Yeah, Yeah!
Gtr. 2
1/2
pp
E5
E(♭5)
Rhy. Fig. 1
End Rhy. Fig. 1
Gtr. 2
mf
P.M.
Riff A
End Riff A
Gtr. 4 (slight dist.)
mf
w/ tremolo

Verse
Gtr. 2: w/ Rhy. Fig. 1
Gtr. 4 tacet
E5
E(♭5)
1. I got these pic - tures, keep on roll - ing 'round my head.
Gtr. 4
pp
E5
E(♭5)
I want to hang them on the wall a - bove my bed. And it's so eas -
Gtr. 2
P.M.
A
E/G♯
- y to step a - side and walk in line like all the rest.
Rhy. Fig. 2
Gtr. 2
*w/ delay
(delay off)
*Set for approximately 5:4 quarter-note regeneration w/ 7 repeats.
Rhy. Fig. 2A
Gtr. 4
mp

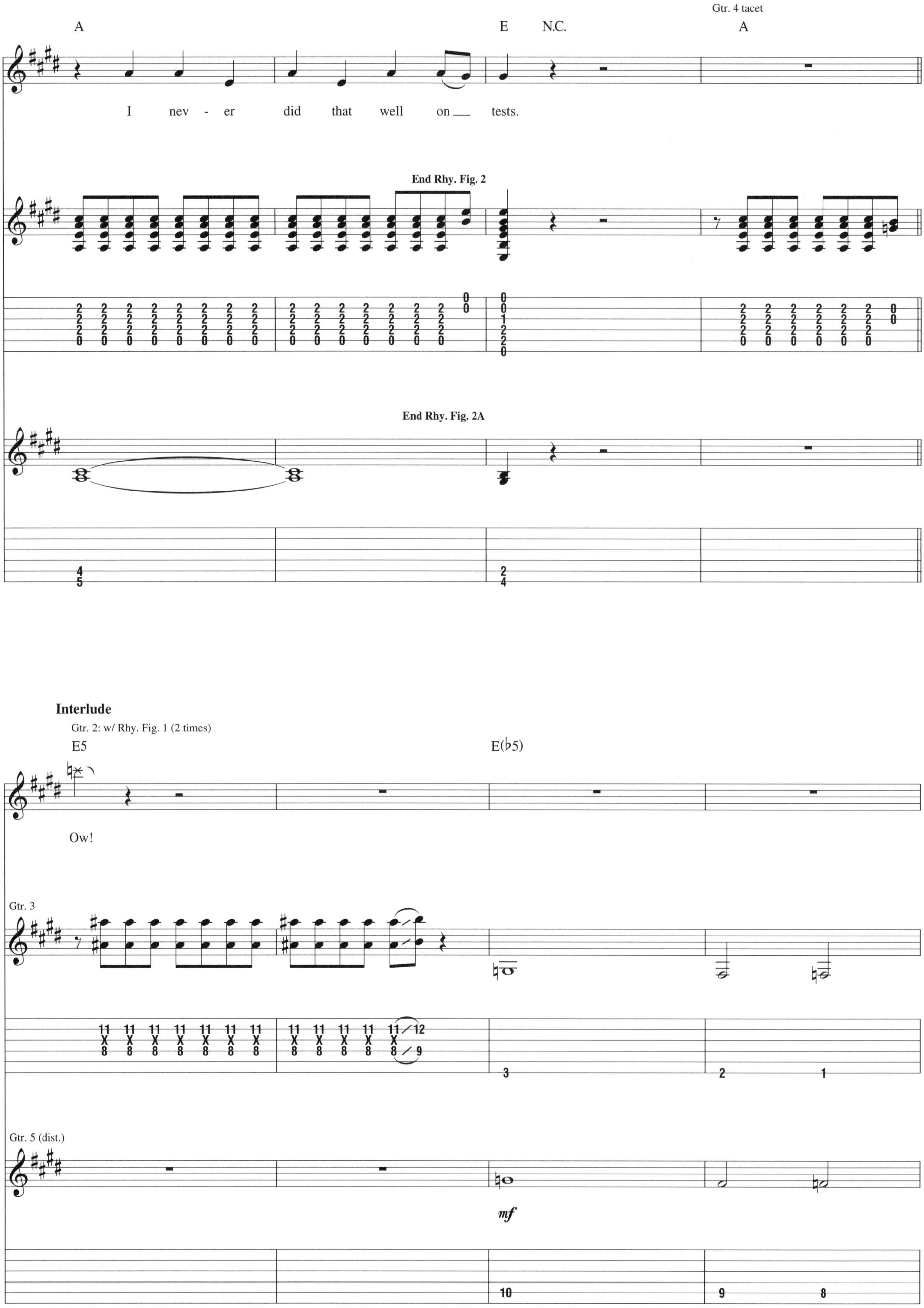
Gtr. 4 tacet
A
E N.C.
A
I nev - er did that well on tests.
End Rhy. Fig. 2
End Rhy. Fig. 2A
Interlude
Gtr. 2: w/ Rhy. Fig. 1 (2 times)
E5
E(♭5)
Ow!
Gtr. 3
Gtr. 5 (dist.)
mf

E5
E(♭5)
1/4
w/ bar
slack
Verse
Gtr. 2: w/ Rhy. Fig. 1 (2 times)
Gtr. 5 tacet
Gtr. 3 tacet
E5
E(♭5)
2. I don't watch T V 'cause it's just a box of lies.
Gtr. 3
E5
E(♭5)
It makes me want to stick a tooth - pick in my mind. While the world
Gtrs. 2 & 4: w/ Rhy. Figs. 2 & 2A
A
E/G♯
goes down the drain, I eat my pop - corn from the bag,
A
uh. Some peo - ple say that I've gone

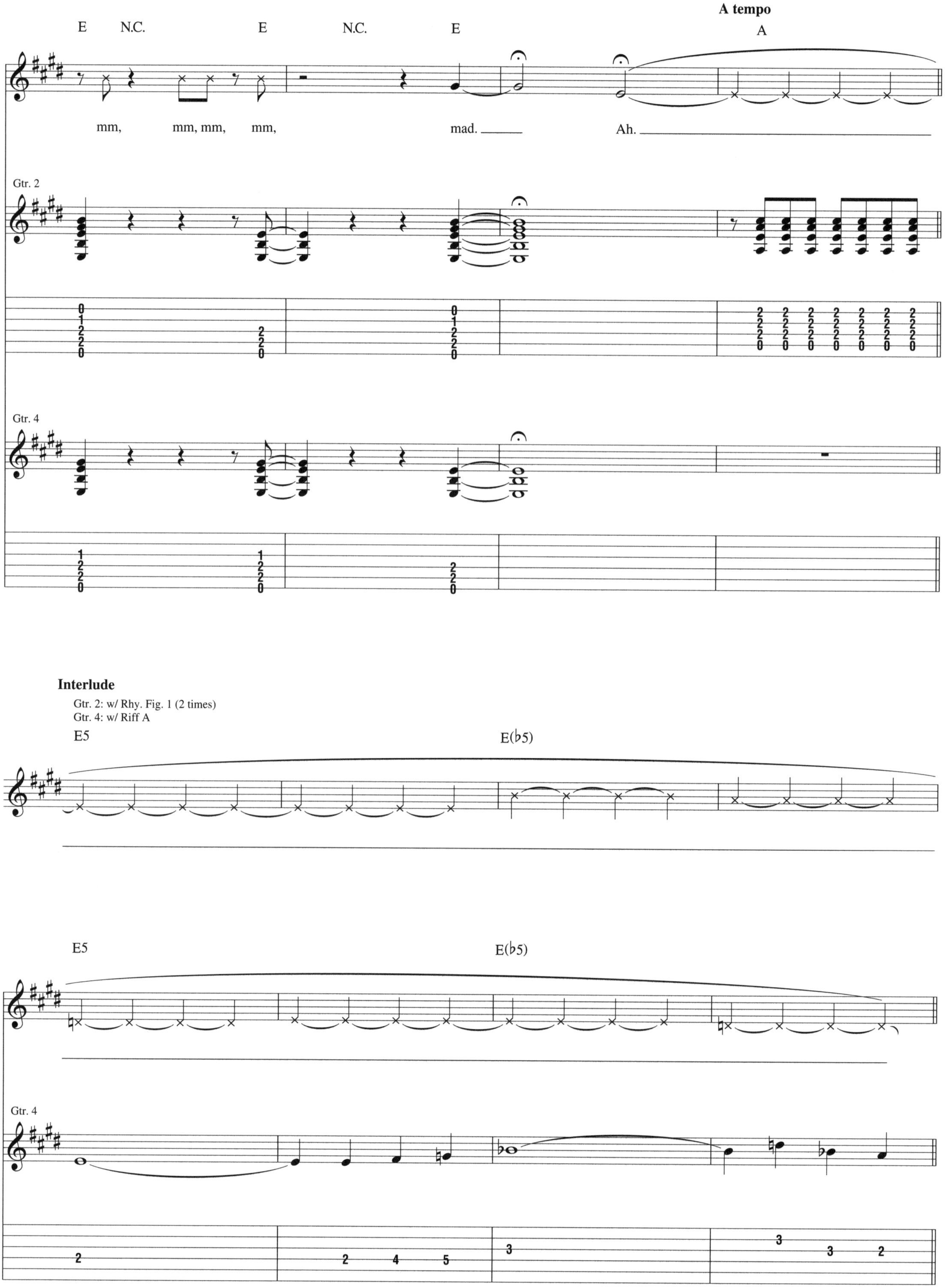
A tempo
E
N.C.
E
N.C.
E
A
mm,
mm, mm,
mm,
mad.
Ah.
Gtr. 2
Gtr. 4
Interlude
Gtr. 2: w/ Rhy. Fig. 1 (2 times)
Gtr. 4: w/ Riff A
E5
E(♭5)
E5
E(♭5)
Gtr. 4

E5
E(♭5)
E5
E(♭5)
Gtr. 3
1/2
1
Gtr. 5
Gtr. 2
P.M.
P.M.
P.M.
P.M.
Gtrs. 3 & 5 tacet
G
G♭
A
A♭
B
B♭
D♭
C
Screamed:
Ah!
Ah!
Ay.
Rhy. Fig. 3
End Rhy. Fig. 3
*Gtrs. 2 & 4
*Composite arrangement
B♭5
Ah!
Ay.

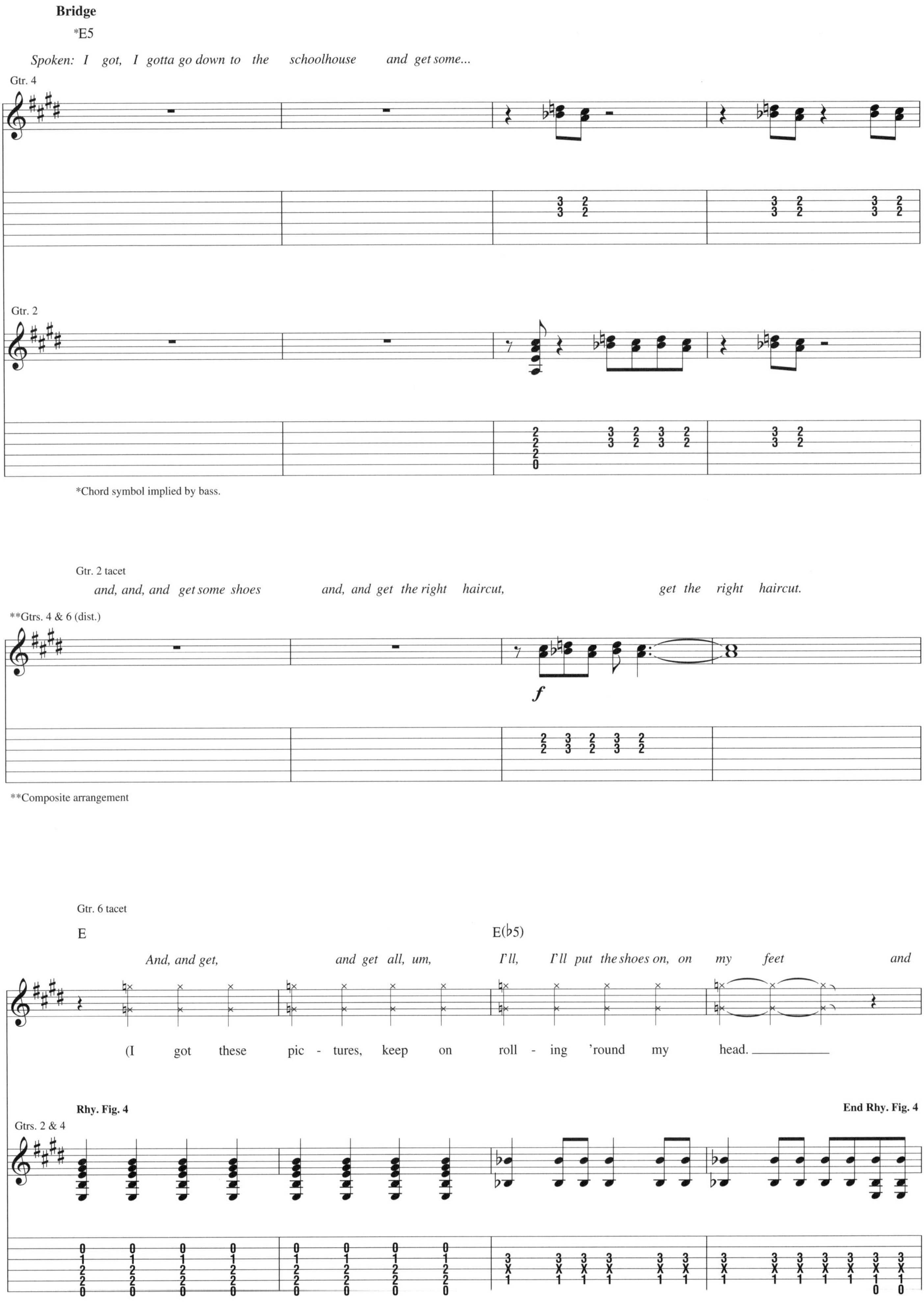
Bridge
*E5
Spoken: I got, I gotta go down to the schoolhouse and get some...
Gtr. 4
Gtr. 2
*Chord symbol implied by bass.
Gtr. 2 tacet
and, and, and get some shoes and, and get the right haircut, get the right haircut.
**Gtrs. 4 & 6 (dist.)
f
**Composite arrangement
Gtr. 6 tacet
E
E(♭5)
And, and get, and get all, um, I'll, I'll put the shoes on, on my feet and
(I got these pic - tures, keep on roll - ing 'round my head.
Rhy. Fig. 4
End Rhy. Fig. 4
Gtrs. 2 & 4

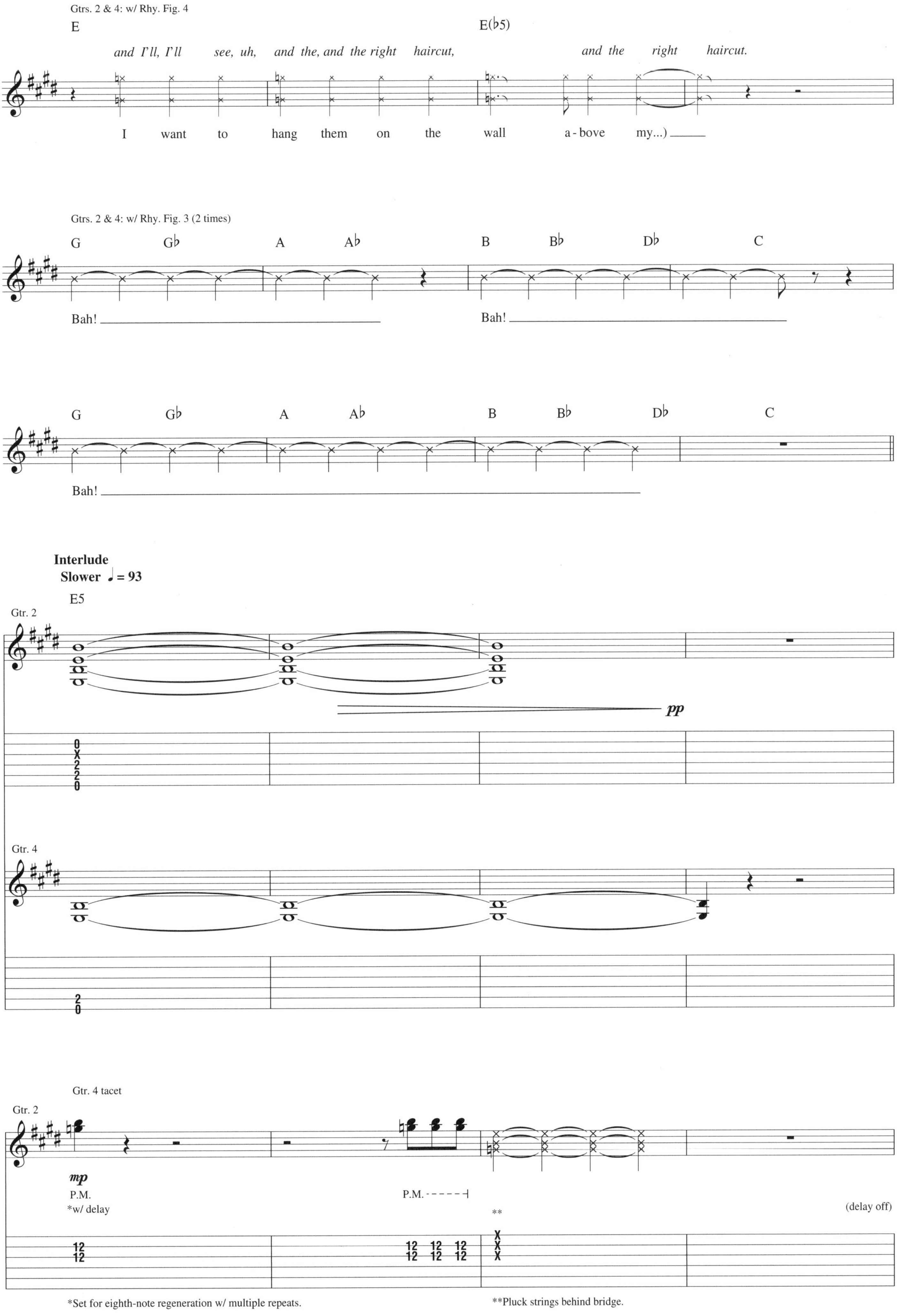
Gtrs. 2 & 4: w/ Rhy. Fig. 4
E
E(♭5)
and I'll, I'll see, uh, and the, and the right haircut, and the right haircut.
I want to hang them on the wall a-bove my...)
Gtrs. 2 & 4: w/ Rhy. Fig. 3 (2 times)
G G♭ A A♭ B B♭ D♭ C
Bah!
Bah!
G G♭ A A♭ B B♭ D♭ C
Bah!
Interlude
Slower ♩ = 93
E5
Gtr. 2
pp
Gtr. 4
Gtr. 4 tacet
Gtr. 2
mp
P.M.
*w/ delay
P.M.
**
(delay off)
*Set for eighth-note regeneration w/ multiple repeats.
**Pluck strings behind bridge.

Gtr. 2
f
mf
**Vol. swell
Gtr. 4
*pp
fdbk.
fdbk.
f
let ring
Pitch: G
*Vol. swell
let ring
1/2
***
1/2
†fdbk.
***Bend string behind nut.
Pitch: G
†Open strings sound through sympathetic vibration.
hold bend
let ring
1/4
w/ bar
-1/2
-1/2
-1 1/2

*Microphonic fdbk., not caused by string vibration.

Outro

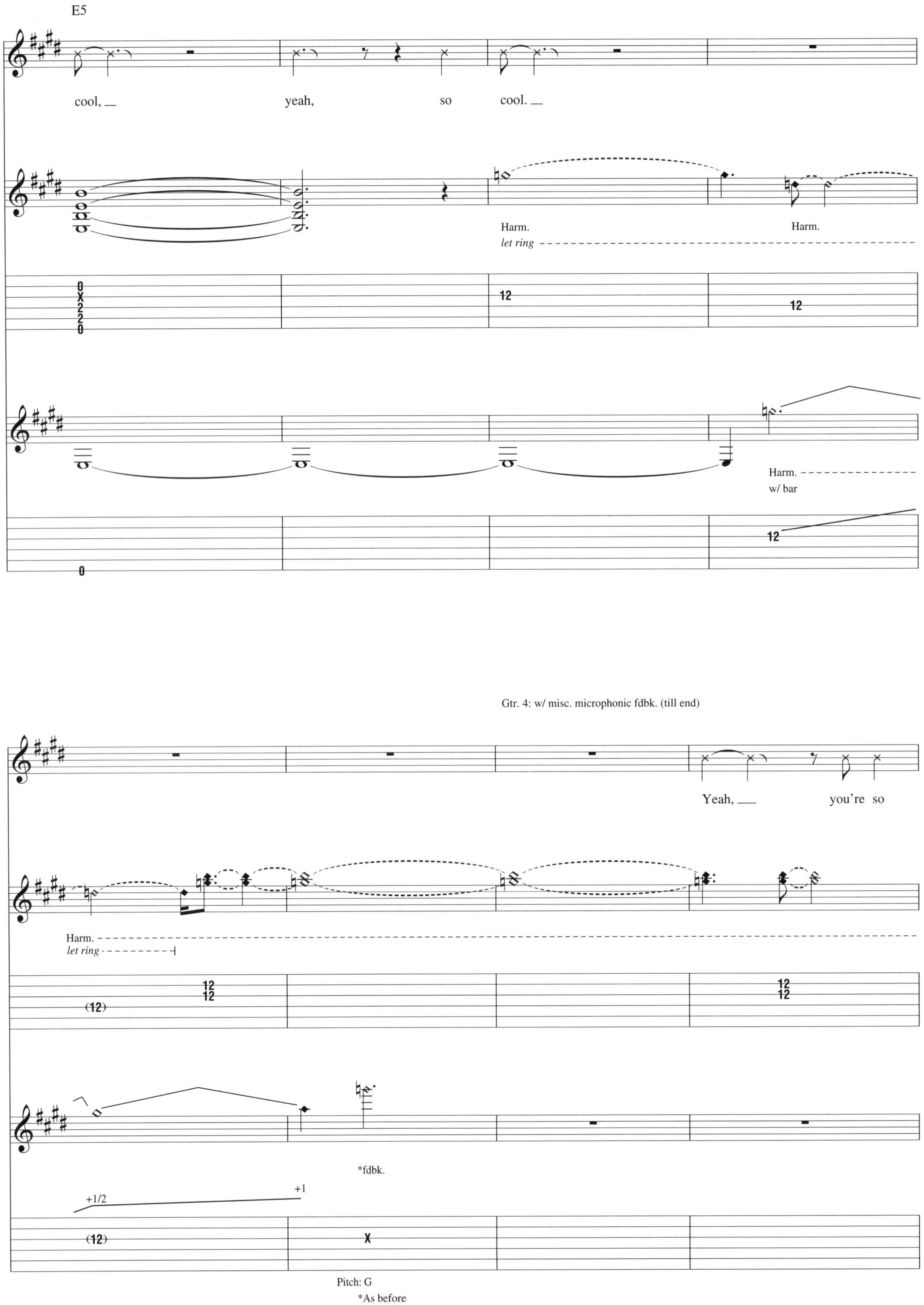
E5
cool, __ yeah, so cool. __
Harm.
let ring
Harm.
0
X
2
2
0
12
12
0
Harm.
w/ bar
12
Gtr. 4: w/ misc. microphonic fdbk. (till end)
Yeah, __ you're so
Harm.
let ring
(12)
12
12
12
12
*fdbk.
+1/2
+1
(12)
X
Pitch: G
*As before

**Microphonic fdbk., not caused by string vibration.
***Open strings sound by sympathetic vibration.
†Tap back of headstock, simulating attack.

Shake Me Down

Words and Music by Brad Shultz, Daniel Tichenor, Jared Champion, Lincoln Parish and Matt Shultz

Copyright © 2010 Sony/ATV Music Publishing LLC, R And R Nomad Music Publishing Co. and 4U2ASKY Entertainment Inc.
All Rights on behalf of Sony/ATV Music Publishing LLC and R And R Nomad Publishing Co.
Administered by Sony/ATV Music Publishing LLC, 8 Music Square West, Nashville, TN 37203
International Copyright Secured All Rights Reserved

B♭ Dm B♭ Dm B♭ Dm
Soft - ly lay - ing on the ground, oo. Not a lot of peo - ple left a - round.
B♭ Dm B♭ Dm B♭ Dm
Oo, oo. In my life, I've seen
End Riff C
mf
Gm Cm B♭ Dm Gm Cm
people walk - ing to the sea just to find mem-o - ries, plagued by con - stant mis - er -
B♭ Dm Gm Cm B♭ Dm Gm Cm
y. Their eyes cast down, fixed up - on the ground. Their eyes cast down.

*Doubled throughout

**Amp tremolo set to sixteenth-note rate w/ heavy depth.

Gtrs. 5 & 6: w/ Rhy. Figs. 1 & 1A (2 times)
B♭ Dm Gm Cm
sheets. Taste the blood, broken dreams. Lone-ly times, in-
B♭ Dm Gm Cm
deed. With eyes cast down, fixed up-on the
Gtr. 3
8va
*w/ DigiTech Whammy Pedal
*Set for one octave above in toe down position.
Gtr. 3 tacet
B♭ Dm Gm
Gtr. 6
ground, their eyes cast down.
Gtr. 3
8va
(Whammy Pedal off)
Gtr. 5
w/ tremolo
w/ tremolo
w/ tremolo

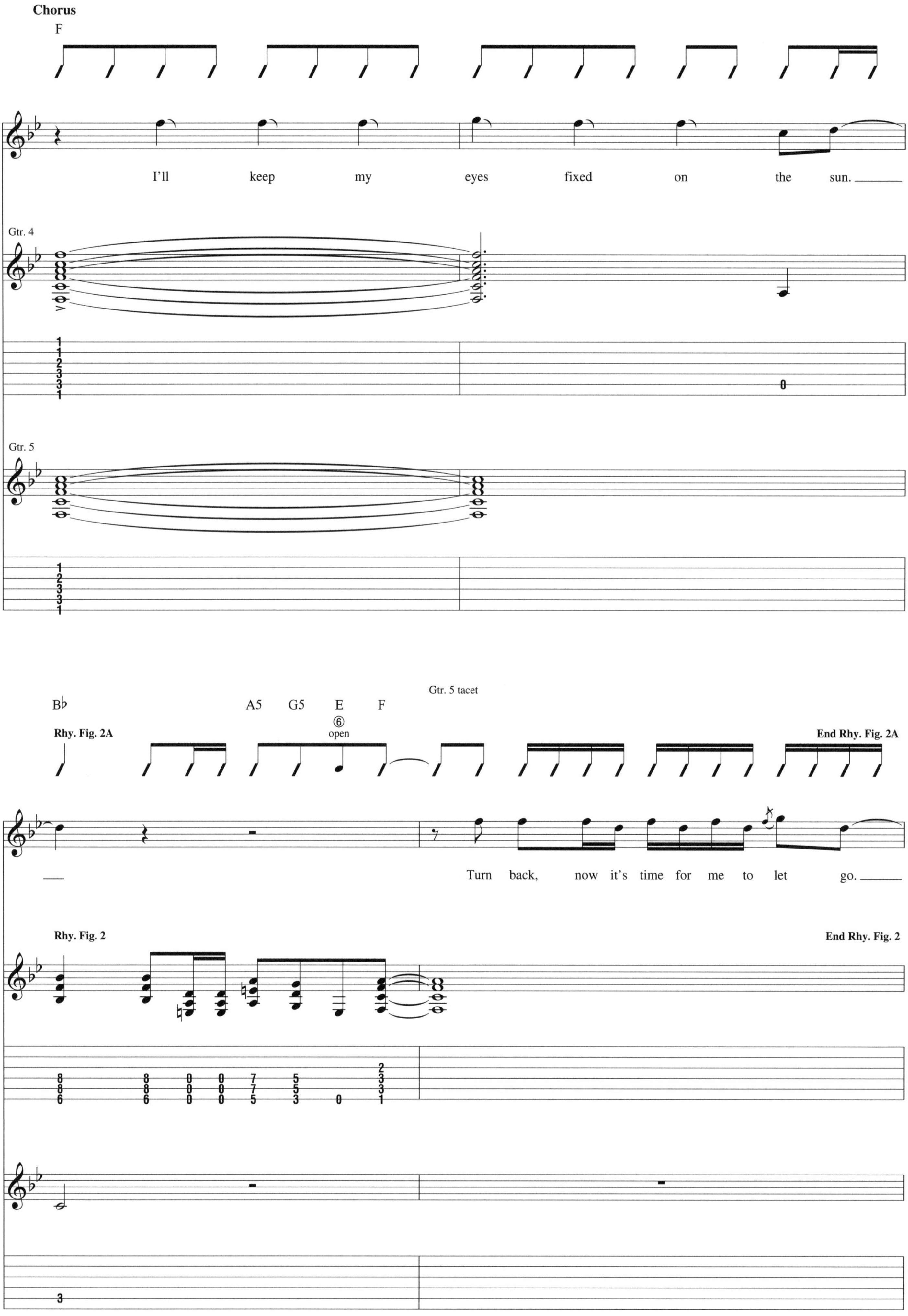
Chorus
F
I'll keep my eyes fixed on the sun.
Gtr. 4
Gtr. 5
B♭
A5 G5 E F
Gtr. 5 tacet
⑥ open
Rhy. Fig. 2A
End Rhy. Fig. 2A
Turn back, now it's time for me to let go.
Rhy. Fig. 2
End Rhy. Fig. 2

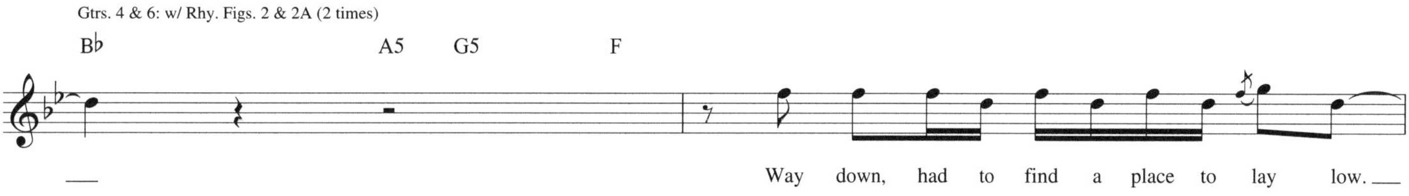

Pitch: B

*Microphonic fdbk., not caused by string vibration.

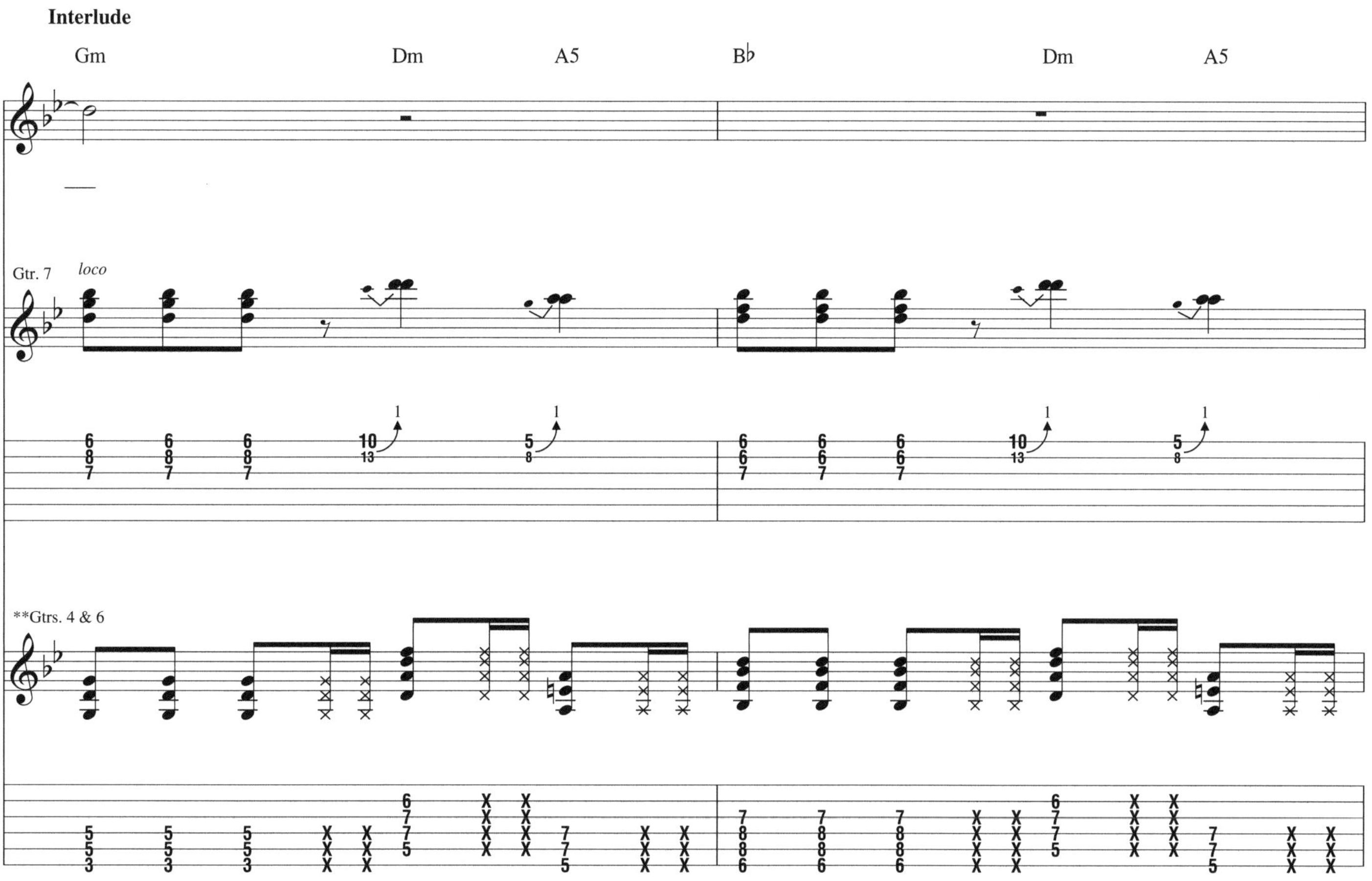

**Composite arrangement

B♭
Dm
A5
Gm
A5
B♭
Dm
A5
B♭
Dm
A5
B♭
Dm
A5
G5
(Gtr. 6, cont. in slashes)

Bridge
F Gm B♭
Rhy. Fig. 3A
End Rhy. Fig. 3A
Gtr. 6
Walk a - round the cor - ner, nev - er saw it com - ing. Still, I
Riff D
End Riff D
Gtr. 7
let ring
let ring
Gtr. 4
Rhy. Fig. 3
End Rhy. Fig. 3
Gtrs. 4 & 6: w/ Rhy. Figs. 3 & 3A (2 times)
Gtr. 7: w/ Riff D (2 times)
tried to make a move. It al - most stopped me from be - lief. I don't
wan - na know the fu - ture, I'm like roll - ing thun - der.
E♭ B♭5 F5 Gm
E - ven on a cloud - y day, e - ven on a cloud - y day.
Gtr. 1
mp
Gtr. 8 (elec.)
mf
w/ fuzz
fdbk.
fdbk.
Pitch: F

Gtr. 8 tacet
E♭
B♭5
F5
G5
E - ven on a cloud - y day,
e - ven on a cloud - y day.
Gtr. 1
Gtr. 1 tacet
E♭5
B♭5
F5
E - ven on a cloud - y day,
e - ven on a cloud - y day,
(Ah,
Gtr. 4
f
Gm
E♭5
B♭5
e - ven on a cloud - y day.
ah.)
Chorus
F
Rhy. Fig. 4
End Rhy. Fig. 4
Gtr. 6
I'll keep my eyes fixed on the...

Gtr. 6: w/ Rhy. Fig. 4 (2 times)
I'll keep my eyes fixed on the... I'll keep my eyes fixed on the sun.
Interlude
Gtr. 1: w/ Riff C (1st 4 meas.)
Gtr. 2: w/ Riff A
B♭ Dm B♭ Dm B♭ Dm B♭ Dm
Gtr. 3
loco
Outro
Gtr. 2: w/ Riff A
Gtr. 3 tacet
B♭ Dm B♭ Dm
Shake me down. Not a lot of peo - ple left a - round.
Gtr. 1
B♭ Dm B♭ Dm B♭
rit.
Oh, oh.
rit.

2024

Words and Music by Brad Shultz, Daniel Tichenor, Jared Champion, Lincoln Parish and Matt Shultz

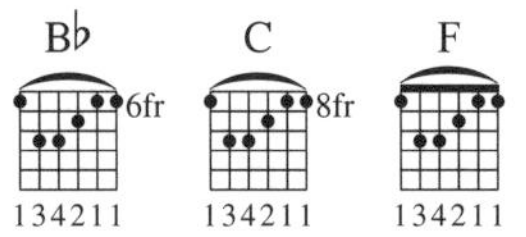

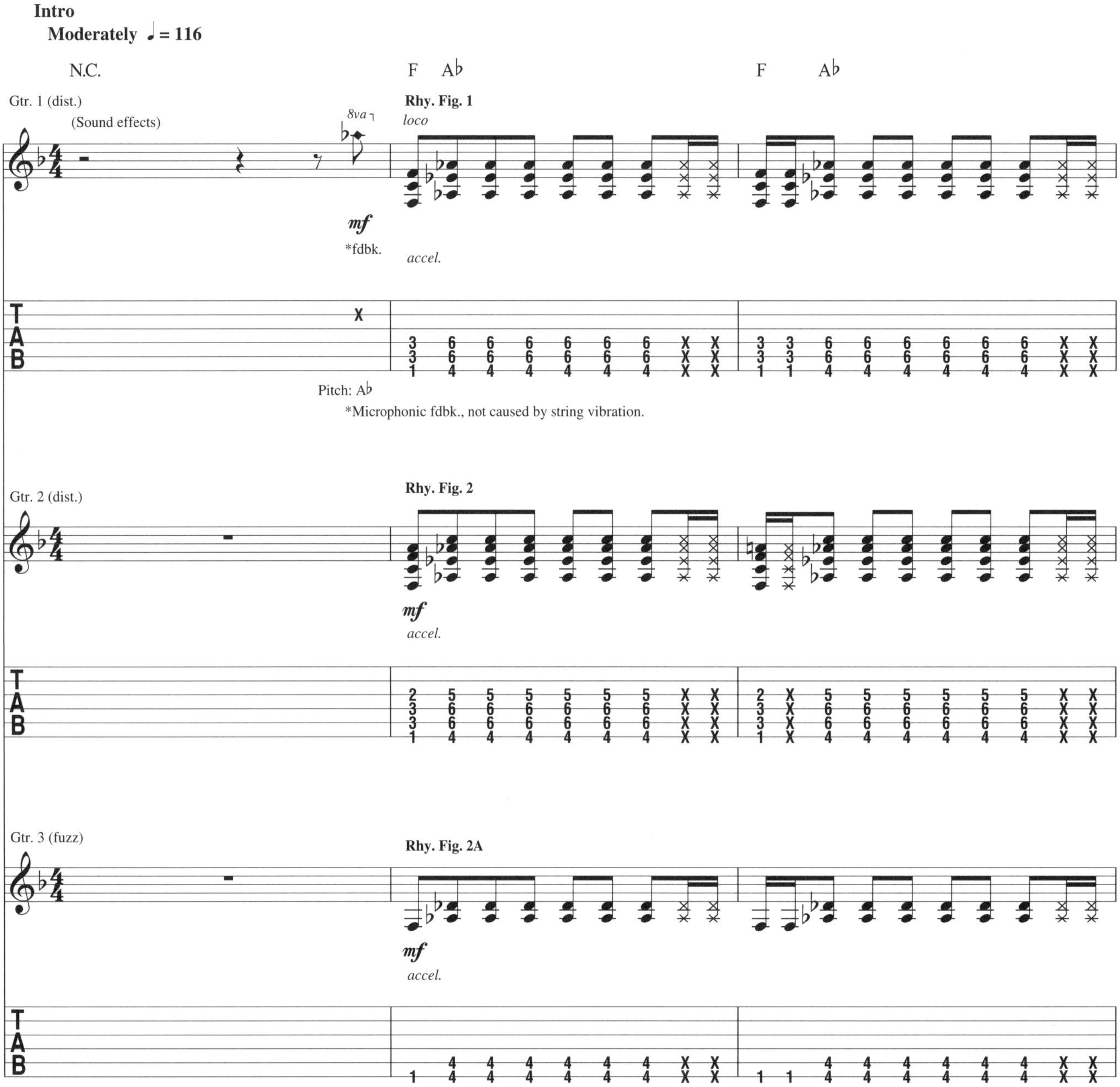

Copyright © 2010 Sony/ATV Music Publishing LLC, R And R Nomad Music Publishing Co. and 4U2ASKY Entertainment Inc.
All Rights on behalf of Sony/ATV Music Publishing LLC and R And R Nomad Publishing Co.
Administered by Sony/ATV Music Publishing LLC, 8 Music Square West, Nashville, TN 37203
International Copyright Secured All Rights Reserved

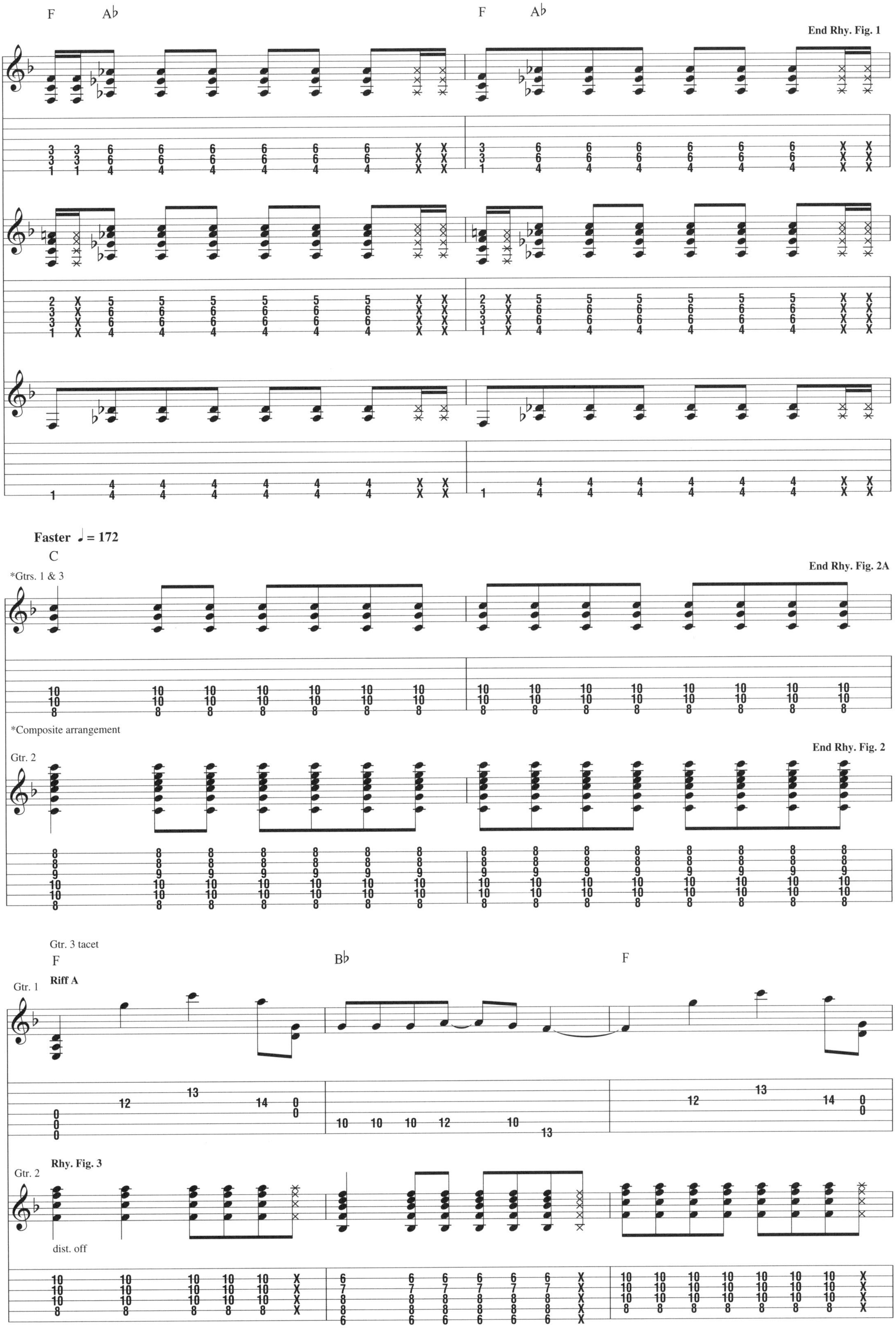
F
A♭
End Rhy. Fig. 1
Faster ♩ = 172
C
*Gtrs. 1 & 3
End Rhy. Fig. 2A
*Composite arrangement
Gtr. 2
End Rhy. Fig. 2
Gtr. 3 tacet
B♭
Gtr. 1
Riff A
Rhy. Fig. 3
dist. off

B♭
F
B♭
End Rhy. Fig. 3
C
End Riff A
Rhy. Fill 1
End Rhy. Fill 1
Verse
Gtr. 1 tacet
Gtr. 2: w/ Rhy. Fig. 3 (1st 4 meas.)
F
B♭
F
B♭
1. Fall in - to that black ___ hole, hon - ey, look - ing up from your eyes. ___
F
B♭
C
Ev - 'ry - thing that you ev - er want - ed. You fight, ___ but why? ___
Gtr. 2
Rhy. Fill 2
End Rhy. Fill 2

Gtr. 2: w/ Rhy. Fig. 3
F
Bb
F
Fold it up just like a piece of pa - per. Take your sweet lit - tle time.
Gtr. 1
Riff B
Bb
F
Bb
You can write it on the side - walk, yeah, but you'll find
Gtr. 2: w/ Rhy. Fill 1
C
it's not right.
End Riff B
Chorus
Bb
C
F
Rhy. Fig. 4
Gtr. 2
And now you're walk - ing through the door
Riff C
let ring
let ring

End Rhy. Fig. 4
B♭
C
just like two thou - sand twen - ty four.
let ring
F
Rhy. Fig. 5
B♭
Said I got to be - lieve.
let ring
C
B♭
End Rhy. Fig. 5
C
Some - day you'll see.
let ring

B♭
C
Some - day you'll see that there's some - thing
End Riff C
let ring
let ring
Interlude
1st time, Gtr. 1: w/ Riff A
Gtr. 2: w/ Rhy. Fig. 3 (1st 4 meas.)
2nd time, Gtr. 1: w/ Riff A (1st 5 meas.)
F
B♭
F
B♭
more, yeah, there's some - thing more. That's why you're so
To Coda
F
B♭
C
bored. Oh, there's some - thing more.
Gtr. 2
Verse
Gtr. 2: w/ Rhy. Fig. 3
F
B♭
F
2. And now he's stand - ing at your front door, no - where bet - ter to be.
B♭
F
B♭
But I can see you tie your own shoe - lac -
Gtr. 1

Gtr. 2: w/ Rhy. Fill 2
C
es, uh, you bleed.
Gtr. 2: w/ Rhy. Fig 3
F
Fall in love just like a
Gtr. 1: w/ Riff B
B♭ F B♭ F
new-born ba - by, blond hair and blue eyes.
Tak-ing pic-tures with your
B♭
Gtr. 2: w/ Rhy. Fill 2
C
Po - la - roid cam - er - a, you'll find it's all right.
Chorus
Gtr. 1: w/ Riff C
Gtr. 2: w/ Rhy. Fig. 4
B♭ C F
And now you're walk - ing through the door
B♭ C
just like two thou - sand twen - ty four.
Gtr. 2
Gtr. 2: w/ Rhy. Fig. 5
F B♭ C B♭
Said I got to be - lieve.
Some - day you'll

C
B♭
C
see.
Some - day you'll see that there's some - thing
Gtr. 2
Interlude
Gtr. 1: w/ Riff A
Gtr. 2: w/ Rhy. Fig. 3
F
B♭
F
B♭
more,
yeah, there's some - thing
more.
That's why you're so
F
B♭
Gtr. 2: w/ Rhy. Fill 2
C
bored.
Oh, there's some - thing
more.
Guitar Solo
Gtr. 2: w/ Rhy. Fig. 3
F
B♭
F
B♭
Gtr. 1
F
B♭
Gtr. 2: w/ Rhy. Fill 2
C
Gtr. 2: w/ Rhy. Fig. 3
F
B♭

F
B♭
1/2
3/4
1/4
1
1 1/4
F
1 1/2
1 3/4
2
2 1/2
Gtr. 2: w/ Rhy. Fill 1
C
2 1/4
Interlude
Slower ♩ = 108
Gtr. 1: w/ Rhy. Fig. 1
Gtrs. 2 & 3: w/ Rhy. Figs. 2 & 2A
F A♭
accel.
Gtr. 1: w/ Rhy. Fig. 2A (last 2 meas.)
D.S. al Coda
Coda
N.C.
rit.
Oh, there's some - thing more.
Gtr. 1
Gtr. 2
*Tape slowed; studio effect.
**Tape slowed; studio effect.

Sell Yourself

Words and Music by Brad Shultz, Daniel Tichenor, Jared Champion, Lincoln Parish and Matt Shultz

Copyright © 2010 Sony/ATV Music Publishing LLC, R And R Nomad Music Publishing Co. and 4U2ASKY Entertainment Inc.
All Rights on behalf of Sony/ATV Music Publishing LLC and R And R Nomad Publishing Co.
Administered by Sony/ATV Music Publishing LLC, 8 Music Square West, Nashville, TN 37203
International Copyright Secured All Rights Reserved

Gtr. 2: w/ Riff A (3 times)
G7
scal - pel in my hand, I'm op - er - at - ing on this rid - dle. Got my
Chok - ing on your can - cer, wait - ing on the new re - leas - es. No more
Gtr. 3 (dist.)
mf
*w/ octaver & chorus
*Octaver set for one octave above.
tongue all tied in knots, on my fore - head placed a la - bel. Took all
need for op - er - a - tors, you al - read - y fooled the mass - es.
2nd time, Gtr. 3: w/ Rhy. Fill 2
my in - spi - ra - tion, carved your name in - to the ta - ble.
Noth - ing left to give you, you al - read - y fooled the mass - es.
let ring
Rhy. Fill 2
Gtr. 3
let ring

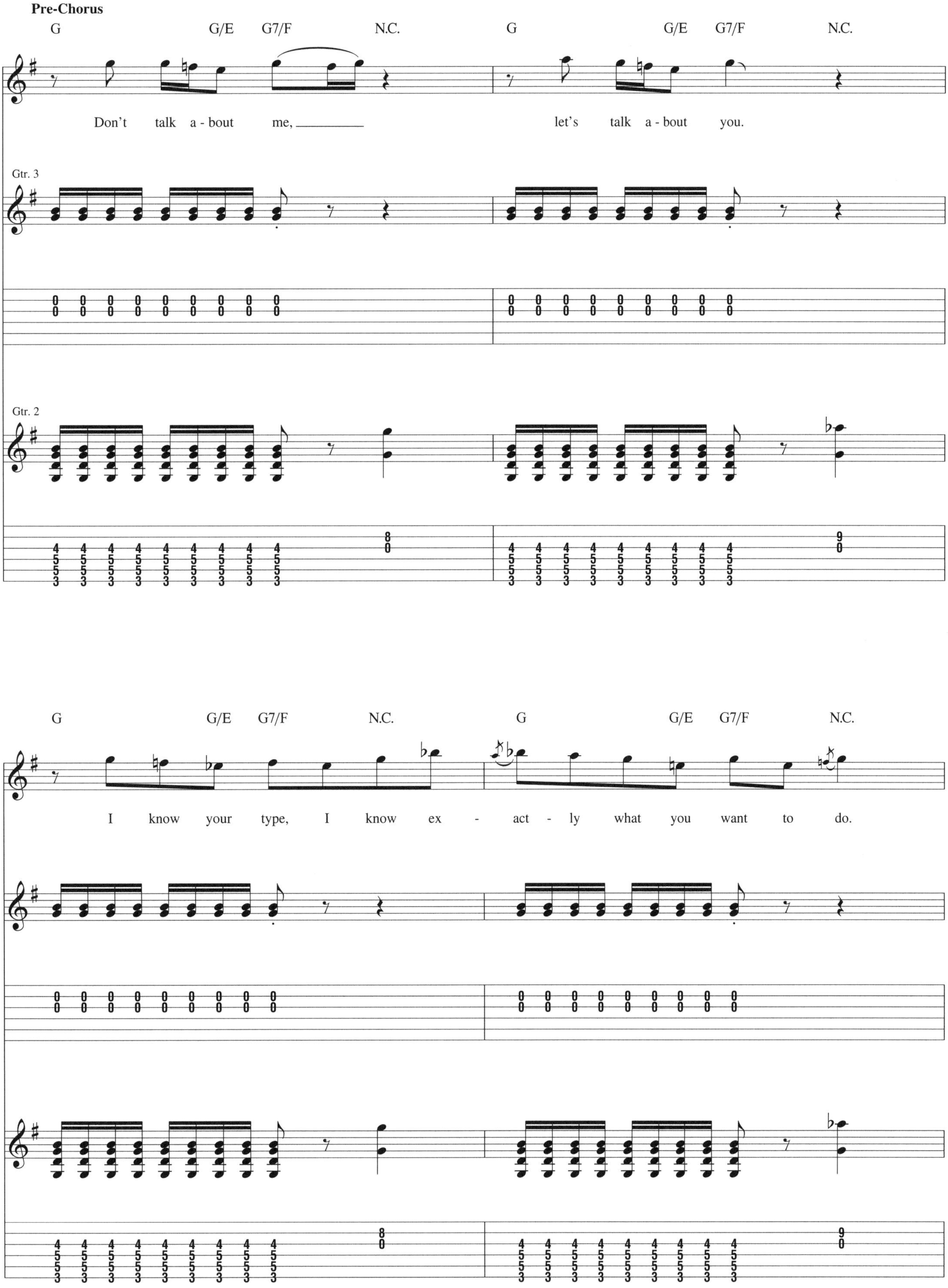
Pre-Chorus
G G/E G7/F N.C. G G/E G7/F N.C.
Don't talk a - bout me, ____ let's talk a - bout you.
Gtr. 3
Gtr. 2
G G/E G7/F N.C. G G/E G7/F N.C.
I know your type, I know ex - act - ly what you want to do.

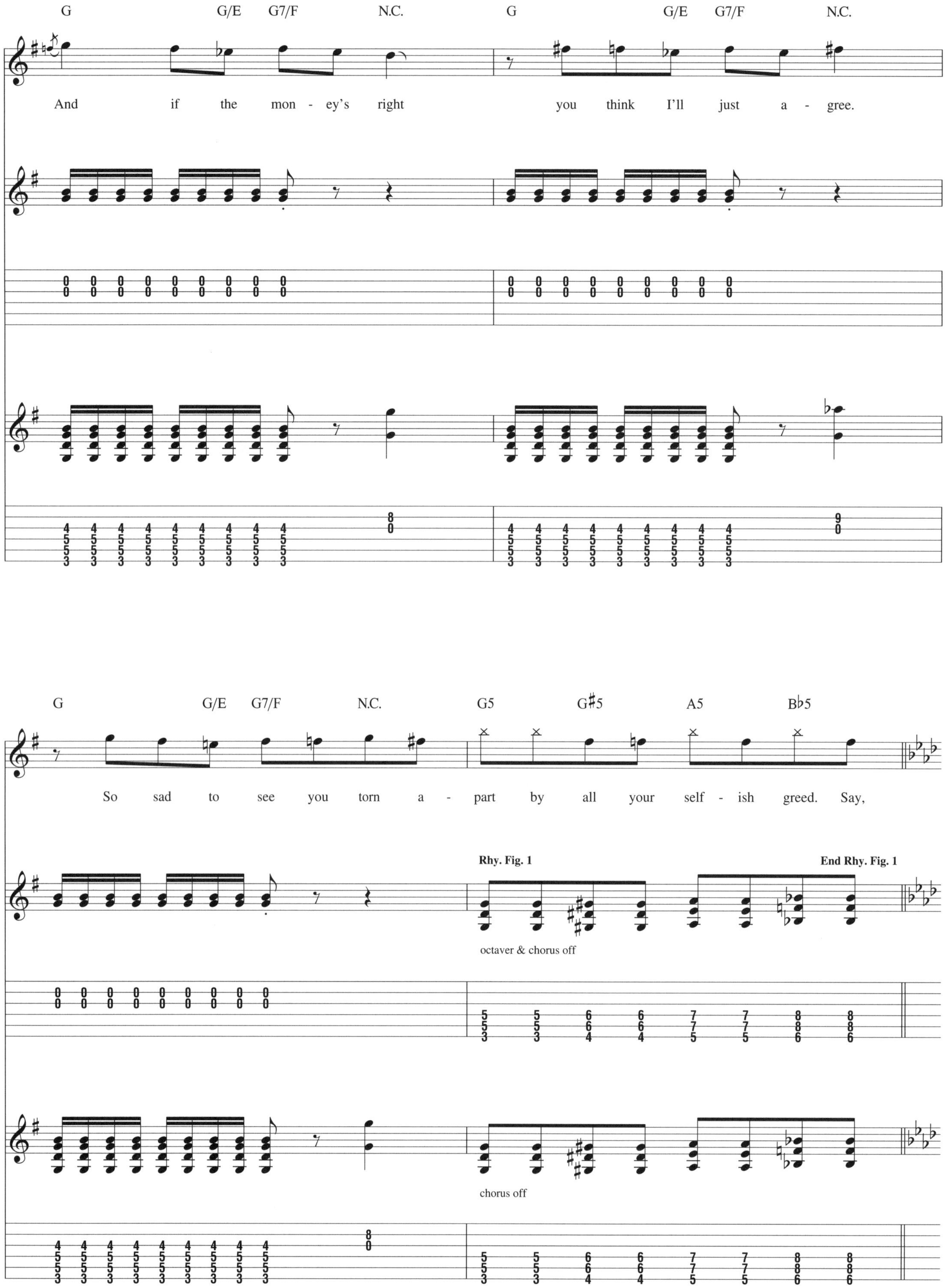
G G/E G7/F N.C. G G/E G7/F N.C.
And if the mon - ey's right you think I'll just a - gree.
G G/E G7/F N.C. G5 G♯5 A5 B♭5
So sad to see you torn a - part by all your self - ish greed. Say,
Rhy. Fig. 1
End Rhy. Fig. 1
octaver & chorus off
chorus off

Chorus
Half-time feel
Bb5 A5 Ab5 G5 Gb5 G5 Ab5
sell your - self, don't be a fool.
Gtrs. 2 & 3
Rhy. Fig. 2
Bb5 A5 Ab5 G5 Gb5 G5 Ab5
Sell your - self, they need a find. You
End Rhy. Fig. 2
1.
End half-time feel
2.
End half-time feel
Gtrs. 2 & 3: w/ Rhy. Fig. 2
Bb5 A5 Ab5 G5 Gb5 G5 Ab5 Bb5 A5 Ab5 G5 Gb5 G5 Ab5 G5 Gb5 G5 Ab5
sell your - self, don't be a fool. Sell your - self. Sell your - self. 2. All my your - self.
Interlude
G7 Gadd2 G7 Gadd2
Gtr. 2
let ring
1/2
Gtr. 3

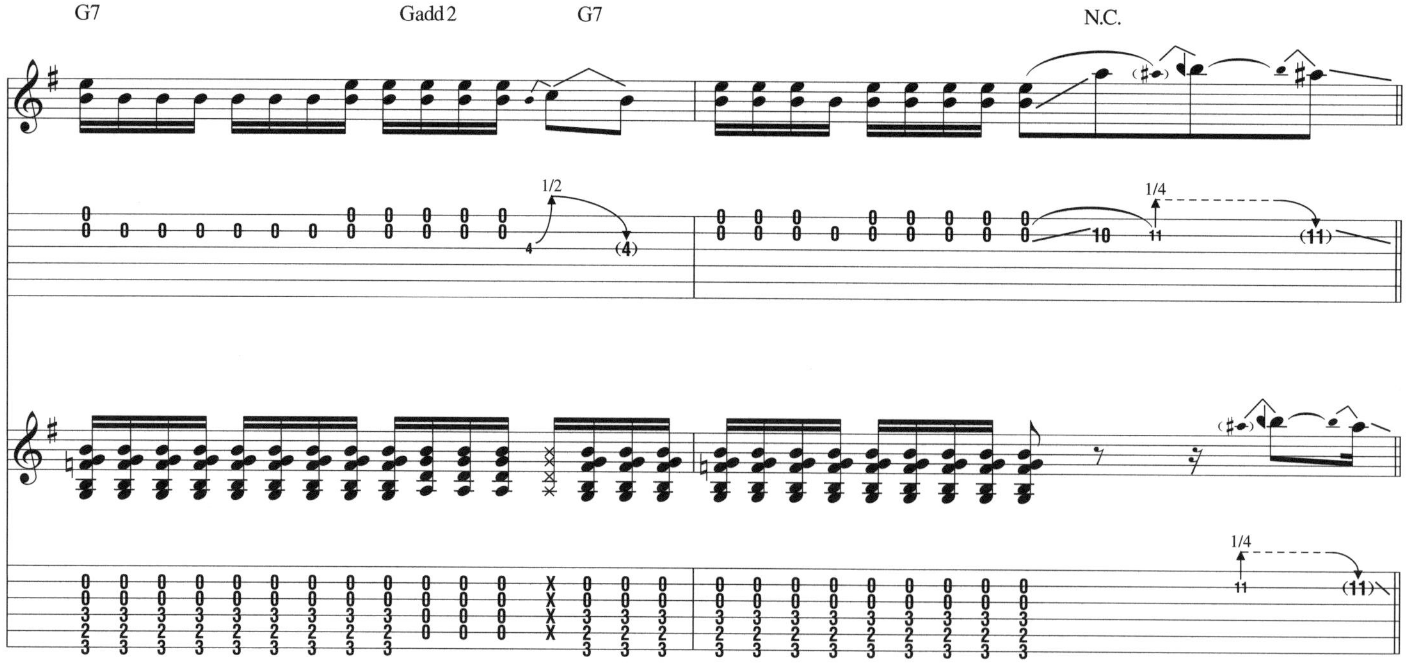
G7
Gadd2
G7
N.C.
1/2
1/4
1/4

Guitar Solo

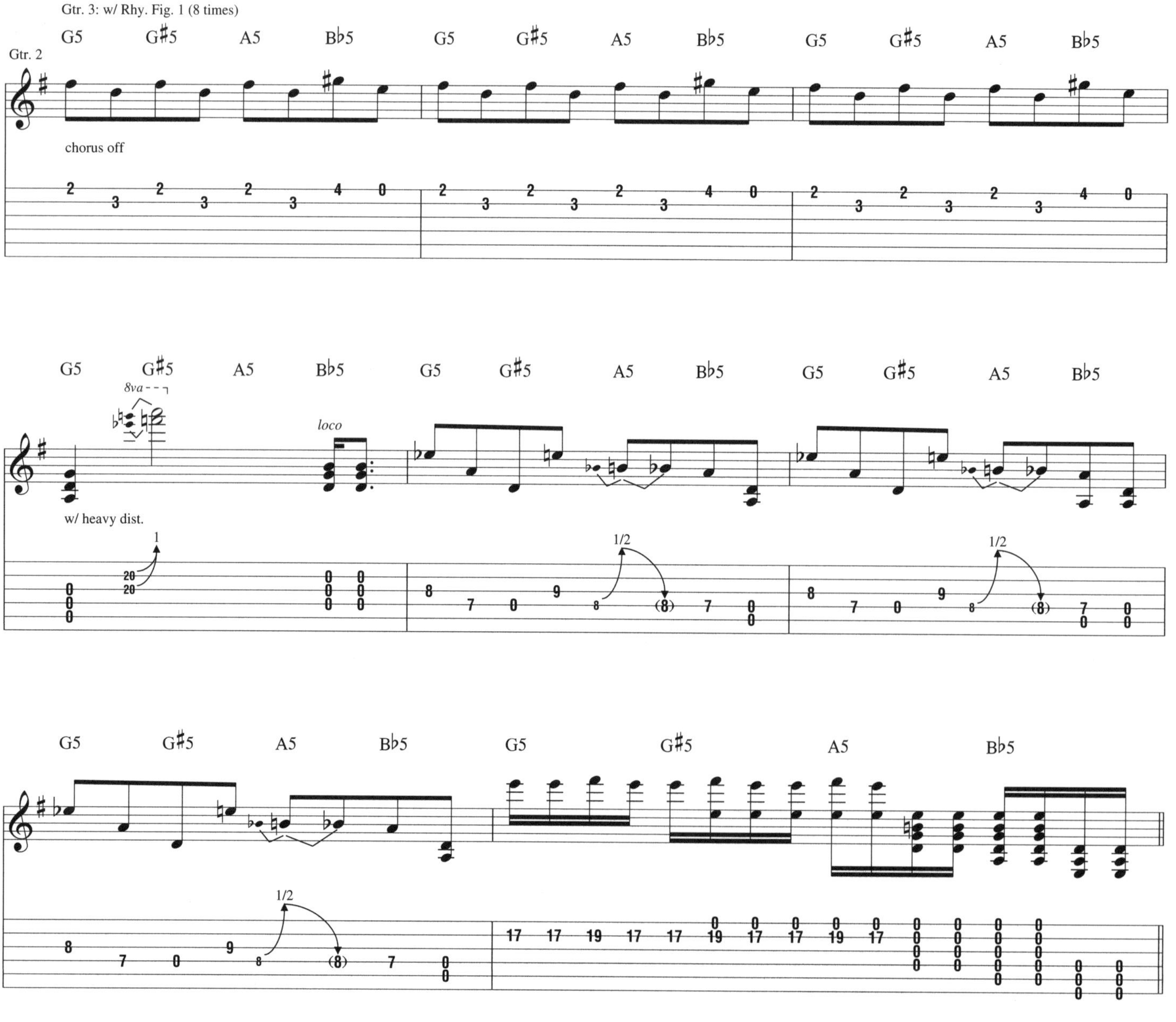
Gtr. 3: w/ Rhy. Fig. 1 (8 times)
G5 G#5 A5 Bb5
Gtr. 2
chorus off
8va
loco
w/ heavy dist.
1
1/2

Interlude

*Set for quarter-note regeneration w/ 11 repeats.

Chorus
Half-time feel
Gtr. 1 tacet
Gtrs. 2 & 3: w/ Rhy. Fig. 2 (2 times)
B♭m Am A♭m Gm G♭m Gm A♭m B♭m Am A♭m Gm G♭m Gm A♭m
Sell your - self, don't be a fool. Sell your - self, they need a find.
Gtr. 4
End half-time feel
B♭m Am A♭m Gm G♭m Gm A♭m B♭m Am A♭m Gm G♭m G5 A♭5
Sell your - self, don't be a fool. Sell your - self. Uh, sell your - self.
Outro
Gtrs. 2 & 3: w/ Rhy. Fig. 1 (3 times)
G5 G♯5 A5 B♭5 G5 G♯5 A5 B♭5 G5 G♯5 A5 B♭5
*w/ delay
*Set for dotted quarter-note regeneration w/ 10 repeats.
G5 G♯5 A5 N.C.
**Increase delay speed to quarter-note regeneration. ***Signal affected in studio.
Gtrs. 2 & 3

Rubber Ball

Words and Music by Brad Shultz, Daniel Tichenor, Jared Champion, Lincoln Parish and Matt Shultz

Copyright © 2010 Sony/ATV Music Publishing LLC, R And R Nomad Music Publishing Co. and 4U2ASKY Entertainment Inc.
All Rights on behalf of Sony/ATV Music Publishing LLC and R And R Nomad Publishing Co.
Administered by Sony/ATV Music Publishing LLC, 8 Music Square West, Nashville, TN 37203
International Copyright Secured All Rights Reserved

B♭
C
give it to the peo - ple, then they'll see, then they'll see.
End Rhy. Fig. 2
Verse
Gtr. 1: w/ Rhy. Fig. 1 (2 times)
F
Am7
2. Spin-ning the tops as the ta - bles, they turn. Made some mis-takes but I still couldn't learn.
Riff A
Gtr. 2 (clean)
mp
End Riff A
Gtr. 2: w/ Riff A
F
Am7
Cov-ered my tracks, thought I was fine. No self-con-trol, now I'm back here in line.
Chorus
Gtr. 1: w/ Rhy. Fig. 2
B♭
F
B♭
All I got is noth-ing but a lit-tle bit of love. You gon-na give it to the peo-ple, then they'll
Interlude
1st time, Gtr. 1: w/ Rhy. Fig. 1 (4 times)
1st time, Gtr. 2: w/ Riff A (4 times)
2nd time, Gtr. 1: w/ Rhy. Fig. 1 (till fade)
2nd time, Gtr. 2: w/ Riff A (till fade)
C
F
Am7
F
see, then they'll see, ah.
They'll see,
Oo,
To Coda
2nd time, D.S. al Coda
Am7
F
Am7
ow.
ah, ha, ha.
(Ah.)
*Synthesized female vocal patch.
Coda
Outro
Play 3 times & fade
F
Am7
F
Am7
Oo, ah, ha, ha.

Right Before My Eyes

Words and Music by Brad Shultz, Daniel Tichenor, Jared Champion, Lincoln Parish and Matt Shultz

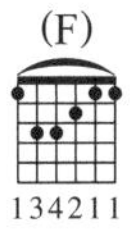

Gtrs. 1-3 & 5-7: Tune down 1/2 step, capo II:
(low to high) E♭-A♭-D♭-G♭-B♭-E♭

Gtr. 4: Drop D tuning, down 1/2 step:
(low to high) D♭-A♭-D♭-G♭-B♭-E♭

Intro
Moderately ♩ = 132

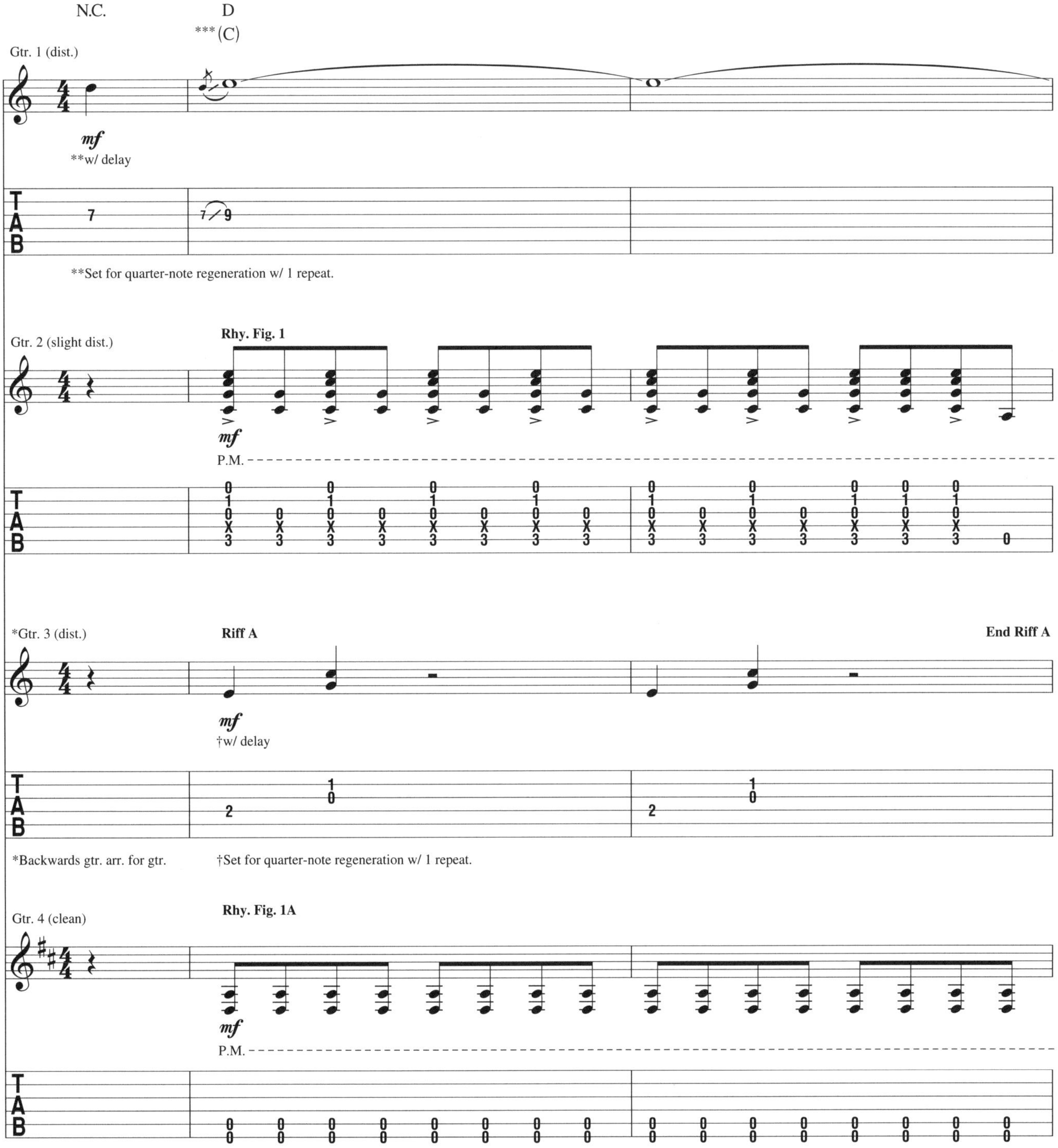

***Chord symbols in parentheses represent chord names respective to capoed guitars.
Capoed fret is "0" in tab. Chord symbols reflect overall harmony.

Copyright © 2010 Sony/ATV Music Publishing LLC, R And R Nomad Music Publishing Co. and 4U2ASKY Entertainment Inc.
All Rights on behalf of Sony/ATV Music Publishing LLC and R And R Nomad Publishing Co.
Administered by Sony/ATV Music Publishing LLC, 8 Music Square West, Nashville, TN 37203
International Copyright Secured All Rights Reserved

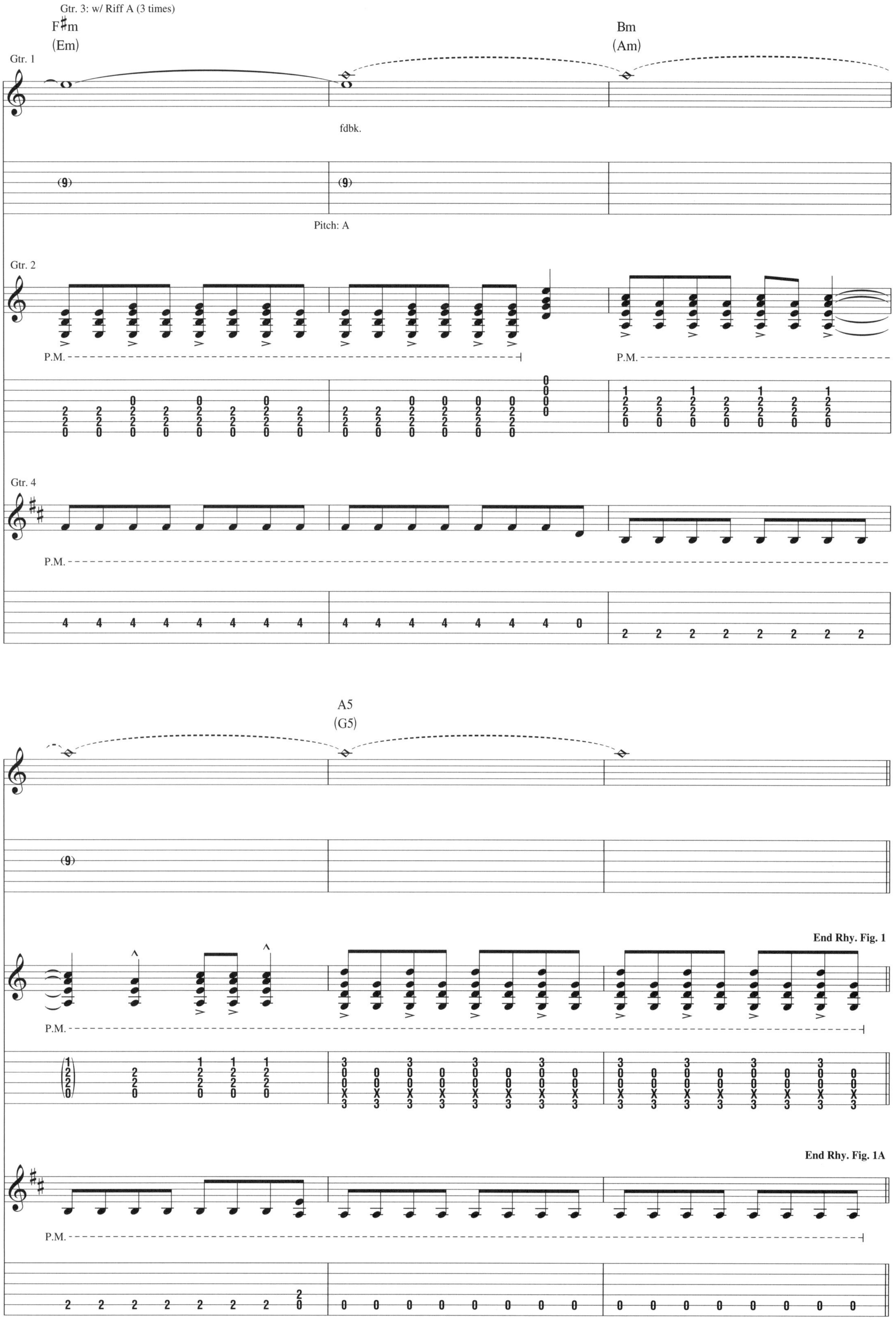
Gtr. 3: w/ Riff A (3 times)
F♯m
(Em)
Bm
(Am)
Gtr. 1
fdbk.
Pitch: A
Gtr. 2
P.M.
Gtr. 4
P.M.
A5
(G5)
End Rhy. Fig. 1
P.M.
End Rhy. Fig. 1A
P.M.

Verse
Gtr. 1 tacet
Gtrs. 2 & 4: w/ Rhy. Figs. 1 & 1A (1 5/8 times)
D (C)
F♯m (Em)
Bm (Am)
1. Tim - ber shakes these trails. They all de - rail, phony, false and frail. An
A5 (G5)
D (C)
empty ocean, lost our way with no direction home. Golden needles,
F♯m (Em)
Bm (Am)
names we take in vain. Find it harder to remain. No,
A5 (G5)
nothing sacred. Still waiting on that explanation.
Gtr. 5 (dist.)
*pp mf
*Vol. swell
Gtr. 2
Rhy. Fill 1
End Rhy. Fill 1
P.M.
Gtr. 4
Rhy. Fill 1A
End Rhy. Fill 1A
P.M.

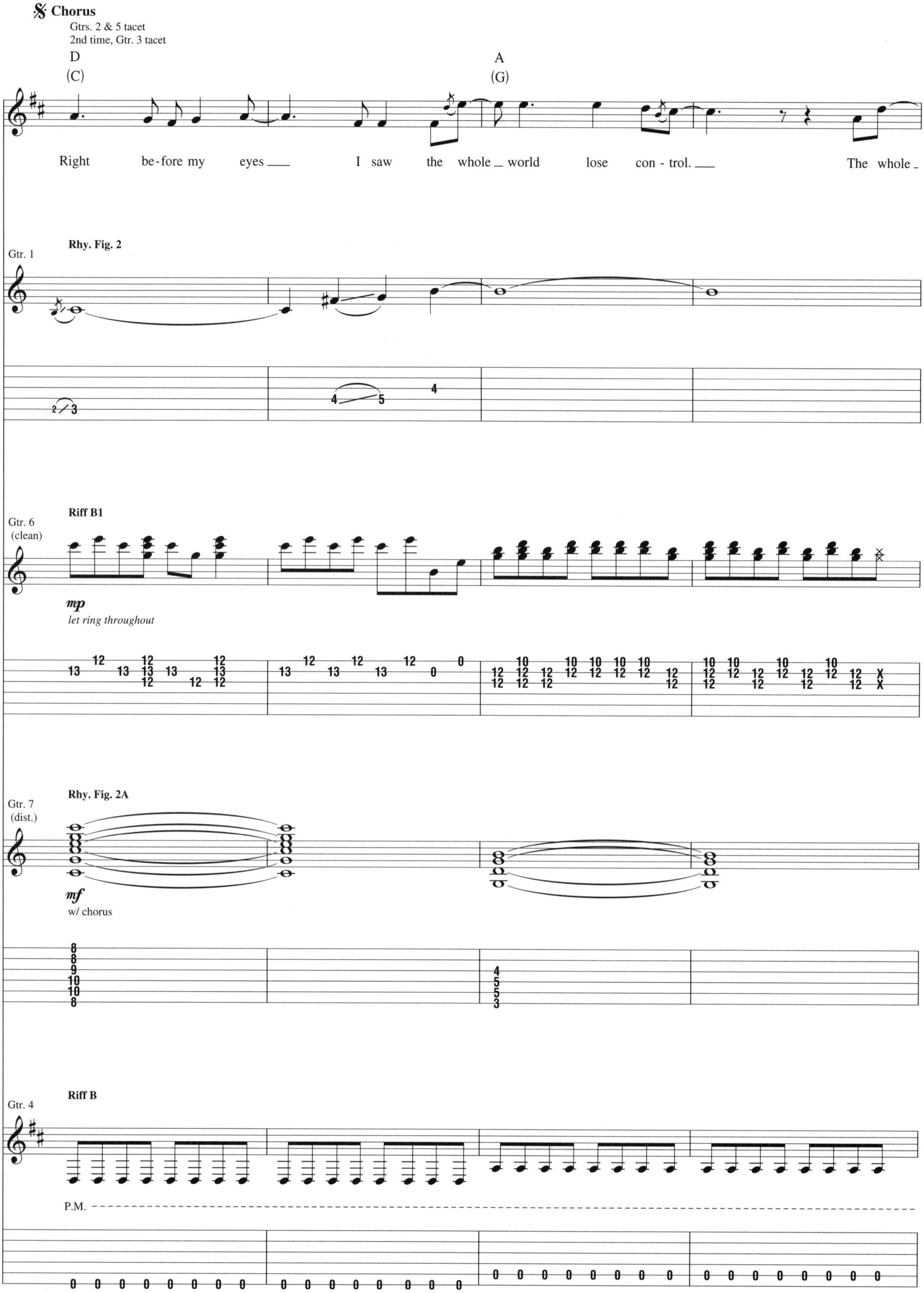
Chorus
Gtrs. 2 & 5 tacet
2nd time, Gtr. 3 tacet
D
(C)
A
(G)
Right be-fore my eyes I saw the whole world lose con-trol. The whole
Gtr. 1
Rhy. Fig. 2
Gtr. 6
(clean)
Riff B1
mp
let ring throughout
Gtr. 7
(dist.)
Rhy. Fig. 2A
mf
w/ chorus
Gtr. 4
Riff B
P.M.

Bm
(Am)
G
(F)
A
(G)
world lost con-trol before my eyes, uh, huh.
End Rhy. Fig. 2
End Riff B1
End Rhy. Fig. 2A
End Riff B
P.M.
Gtr. 1: w/ Rhy. Fig. 2
Gtrs. 4 & 6: w/ Riffs B & B1
1st time, Gtr. 7: w/ Rhy. Fig. 2A (1st 4 meas.)
2nd time, Gtr. 7: w/ Rhy. Fig. 2A
D
(C)
A
(G)
I fell through the floor, I could-n't take it an-y-more. I can't
To Coda
Bm
(Am)
G
(F)
A
(G)
take this an-y-more, it breaks my mind, uh, huh.
Gtr. 7

Verse
Gtrs. 2 & 3: w/ Rhy. Figs. 1 & 1A (2 times)
Gtr. 7 tacet
D
(C)
F♯m
(Em)
2. Hold her dirt - y hands o - ver the flames, get-ting pleas-ure from the pain.
Gtr. 1
Gtr. 7
Bm
(Am)
A
(G)
Soft-ly scream - ing, the pis - tol that you raise has spo - ken.
Gtr. 1
let ring
Gtr. 3
*pp
mf
mp < mf
*Vol. swells

Gtr. 3: w/ Riff A (2 1/2 times)
D
(C)
F♯m
(Em)
Bm
(Am)
Gold-en nee - dles, names we take in vain. __ Find it hard - er to __ re - main. __
Gtr. 1
let ring
let ring
D.S. al Coda
Coda
Gtrs. 2 & 4: w/ Rhy. Fills 1 & 1A
A
(G)
A
(G)
Noth - ing sa - cred. Still wait - ing on that ex - plan - a - tion. ______
Gtr. 1
let ring
Gtr. 3
*pp
mf
*Vol. swell
Gtr. 5

Bridge

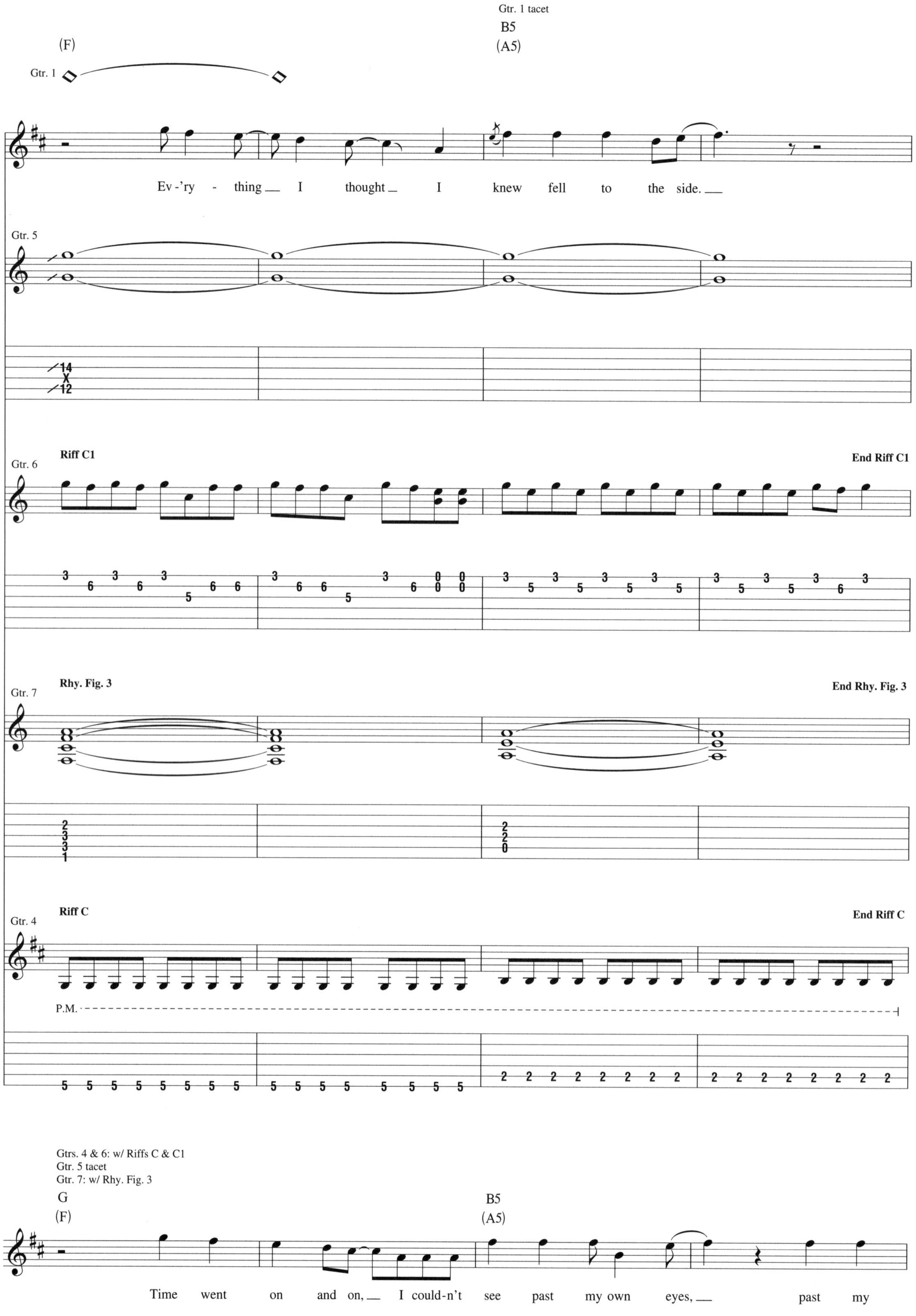
Gtr. 1 tacet
B5
(A5)
(F)
Gtr. 1
Ev-'ry - thing I thought I knew fell to the side.
Gtr. 5
Riff C1
Gtr. 6
End Riff C1
Rhy. Fig. 3
Gtr. 7
End Rhy. Fig. 3
Riff C
Gtr. 4
End Riff C
P.M.
Gtrs. 4 & 6: w/ Riffs C & C1
Gtr. 5 tacet
Gtr. 7: w/ Rhy. Fig. 3
G
(F)
B5
(A5)
Time went on and on, I could-n't see past my own eyes, past my

A
(G)
B5
(A5)
eyes, past my eyes, past my
Gtr. 1
Fill 1
End Fill 1
grad. bend
1/2
Gtr. 6
Gtr. 7
Rhy. Fill 2A
End Rhy. Fill 2A
w/ bar
-1/4
Gtr. 4
Rhy. Fill 2
End Rhy. Fill 2
P.M.
Gtr. 1: w/ Fill 1
Gtrs. 4 & 7: w/ Rhy. Fills 2 & 2A
A
(G)
eyes.
Gtr. 6

Outro-Chorus

Gtr. 1 tacet
D
(C)
A
(G)
I fell through the floor, I could - n't take it an - y - more. I can't
fdbk.
let ring
Pitch: B
P.M.
P.M.
B5
(A5)
G5
(F5)
A5
(G5)
N.C.
rit.
take this an - y - more, breaks my mind, uh, huh.
Gtr. 2
P.M.
rit.
Gtr. 4
rit.
P.M.

Around My Head

Words and Music by Brad Shultz, Daniel Tichenor, Jared Champion, Lincoln Parish and Matt Shultz

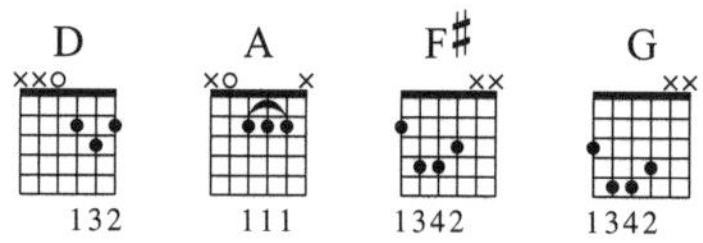

Intro
Moderately ♩ = 110

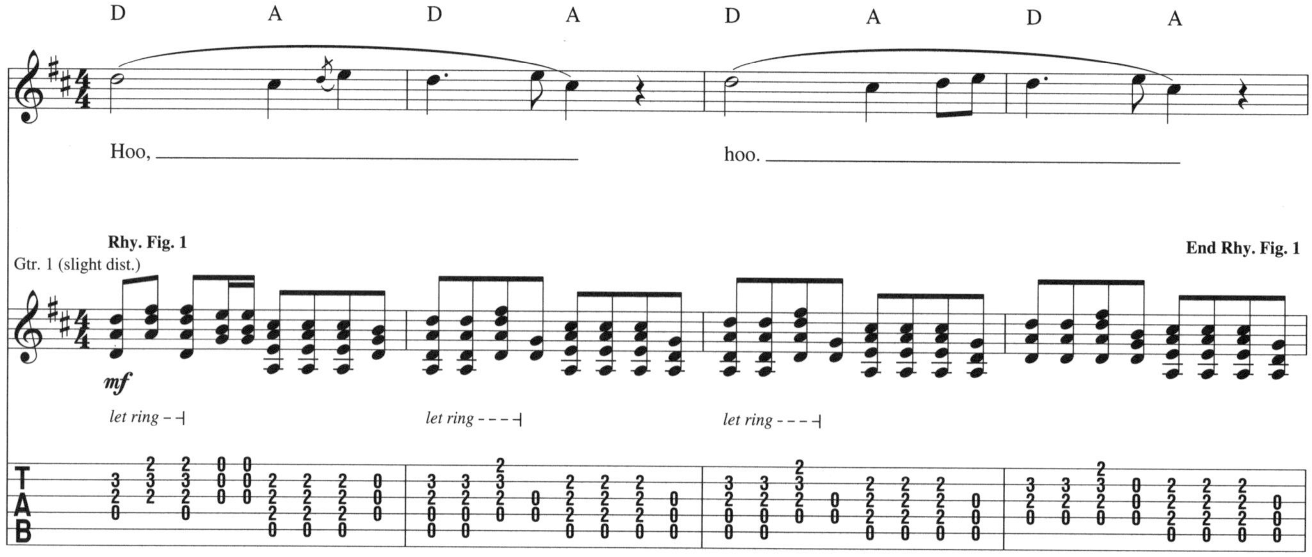

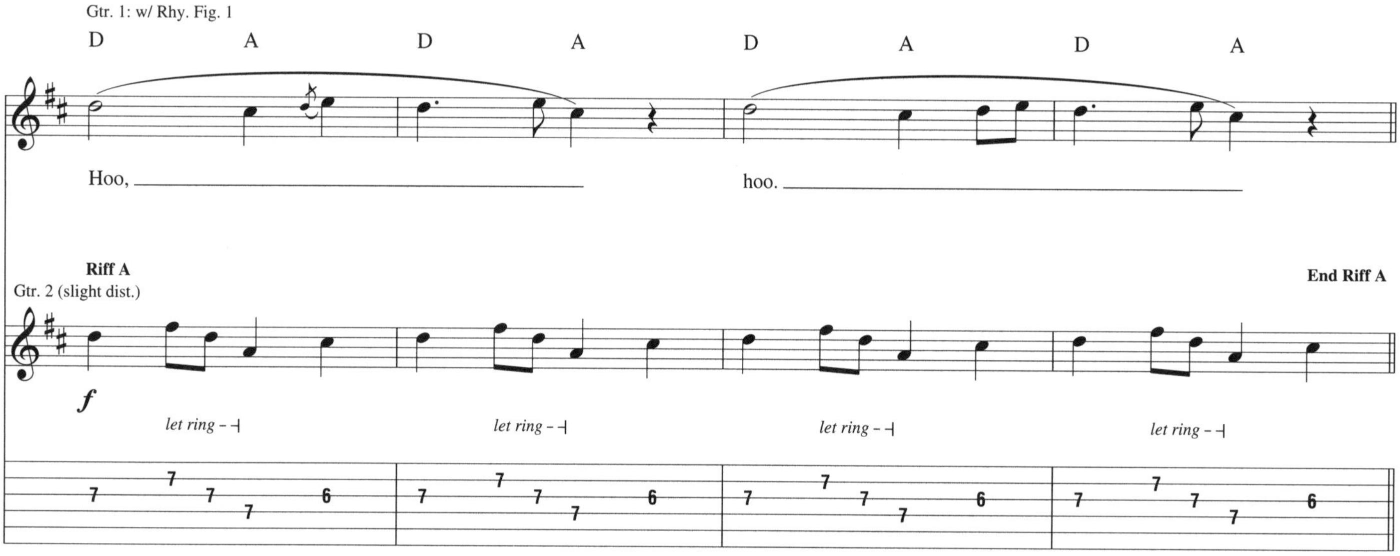

Copyright © 2010 Sony/ATV Music Publishing LLC, R And R Nomad Music Publishing Co. and 4U2ASKY Entertainment Inc.
All Rights on behalf of Sony/ATV Music Publishing LLC and R And R Nomad Publishing Co.
Administered by Sony/ATV Music Publishing LLC, 8 Music Square West, Nashville, TN 37203
International Copyright Secured All Rights Reserved

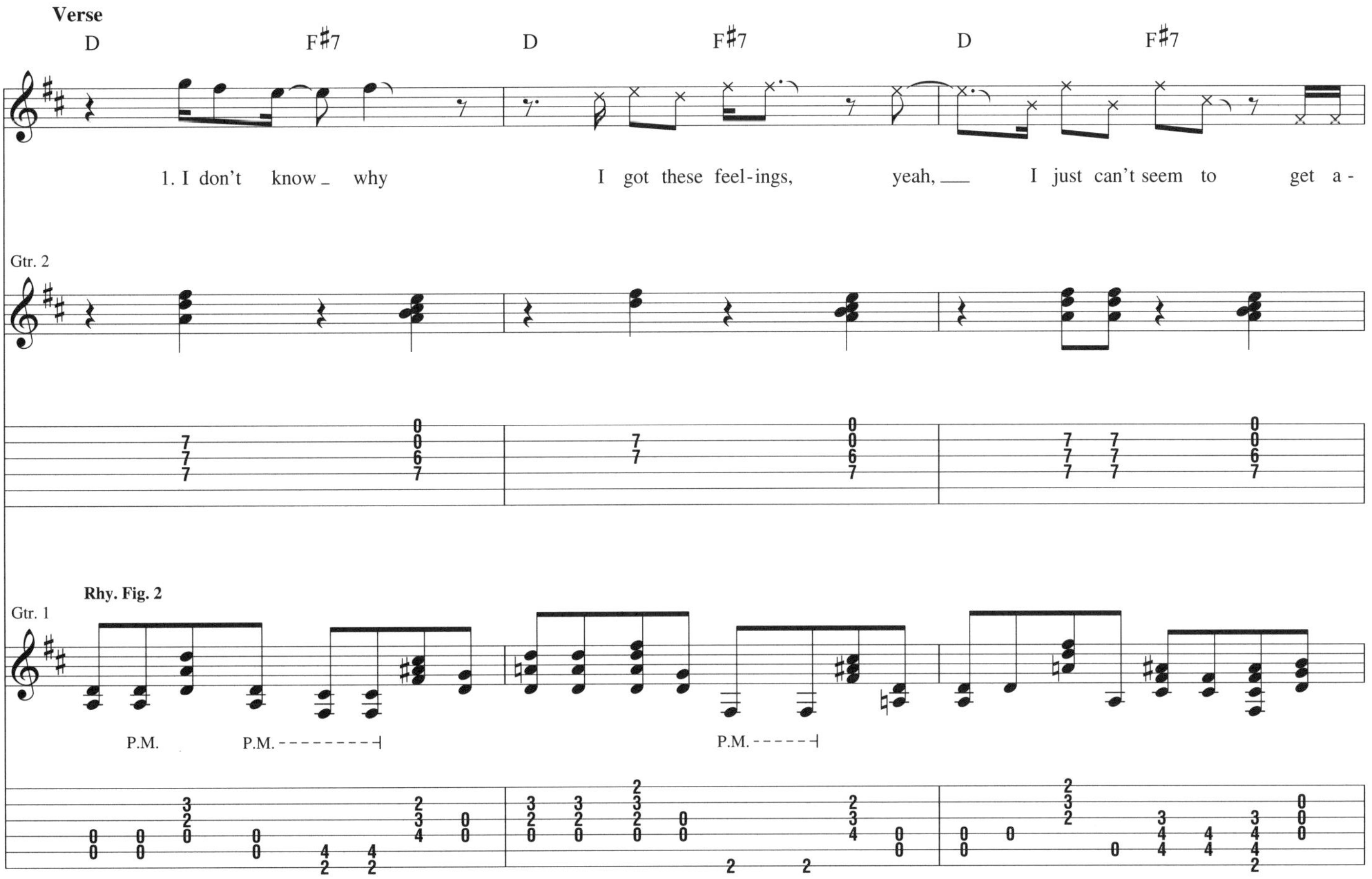
Verse
D
F♯7
D
F♯7
D
F♯7
1. I don't know _ why I got these feel-ings, yeah, ___ I just can't seem to get a -
Gtr. 2
Rhy. Fig. 2
Gtr. 1
P.M.
P.M.
P.M.

G
F♯
D
F♯7
D
F♯7
way from. Can you dig it? You may nev - er see it, no. ____ You won't find it fall-ing off __ my tongue. _
P.M.
P.M.

D F♯7 G A6sus2
I'll tuck it down 'til I fi-n'ly lose it. Oo, oo, oo, oo, ah, ah, ah, ah. Oo, oo, oo, oo, ah, ah, ah, ah.
End Rhy. Fig. 2
Riff B
End Riff B
P.M.
(cont. in slashes)
Chorus
D A F♯ G D A F♯ G
Rhy. Fig. 3
End Rhy. Fig. 3
Gtr. 1
I don't think it's ver-y nice to walk a-round my head all night. You
Gtr. 2
Riff C
End Riff C
let ring
D A F♯ G D A F♯ G
got me tan-gled like a bread tie, twist-ed. I don't think it's fair, do

Interlude
Gtr. 1: w/ Rhy. Fig. 1
Gtr. 2: w/ Riff A
D A D A D A D A
you? Oo.
Verse
Gtr. 1: w/ Rhy. Fig. 2
D F#7 D F#7 D F#7
2. Out here on the flip side, you know I took the long way 'round, 'cause all I real-ly am is a
Gtr. 2
G F# D F#7 D F#7
home-made el - e - va - tor. Blind-ed by your sun-shine, put you on a plane to old Par -
Gtr. 1: w/ Riff B
D F#7 G A6sus2
is. Laid my cards down on the ta - ble. Oo, oo, oo, oo, ah, ah, ah, ah. Oo, oo, oo, oo, ah, ah, ah, ah.

Chorus
Gtr. 1: w/ Rhy. Fig. 3 (2 times)
Gtr. 2: w/ Riff C
D A F♯ G D A F♯ G
I ___ don't think it's ver - y nice to walk _ a - round _ my head all ___ night. You
D A F♯ G D A F♯ G
got me tan - gled like a bread tie, twist - ed. I don't think it's fair. ___
Gtr. 2
let ring
Bridge
F♯5 G5
Can't find a rea - son for these feel - ings cloud - ing up a - bove me.
Riff D
Gtr. 3 (slight dist.)
End Riff D
mf
Rhy. Fig. 4A
Gtr. 2
End Rhy. Fig. 4A
Rhy. Fig. 4
Gtr. 1
End Rhy. Fig. 4

Gtrs. 1 & 2: w/ Rhy. Figs. 4 & 4A (2 times)
Gtr. 3: w/ Riff D (2 times)
F♯5
G5
F♯5
G5
'Cause God, He told me, say He's gon-na send me some-thing love-ly. But e-ven still, at times, I won-der what you're think-ing of me.
F♯5
G5
rit.
F♯5
You're prob-'ly sure I lost my mind, oh mind, oh mind, oh mind, oh mind.
Gtr. 2
rit.
Gtr. 1
rit.
Chorus
A tempo
Gtr. 2 tacet
D
A
F♯
G
I don't think it's ver-y nice to
Rhy. Fig. 5
End Rhy. Fig. 5
Gtr. 1
Gtr. 1: w/ Rhy. Fig. 5 (3 times)
D
A
F♯
G
D
A
walk a-round my head all night. You got me tan-gled like a

F♯ G D A F♯ G
bread tie, twist - ed. I don't think it's fair.
8va
Gtr. 2
mf
*fdbk.
Pitch: D G♯ A G D
*Microphonic fdbk., not caused by string vibration.
Gtr. 1: w/ Rhy. Fig. 3 (2 times)
Gtr. 2: w/ Riff C (1 1/2 times)
D A F♯ G D A
I don't think it's ver - y po - lite to walk a - round my
Voc. Fig. 1
(Do, do, do. Do, do, do Do, do, do.
F♯ G D A F♯ G
head all night. You got me tan - gled like a bread tie, twist - ed.
End Voc. Fig. 1
Do, do, do. Do, do, do. Do, do, do.)
D A F♯ G
I don't think it's fair.
Gtr. 2
f
let ring
let ring

Outro

Bkgd. Voc.: w/ Voc. Fig. 1
Gtr. 1: w/ Rhy. Fig. 3 (1st 3 meas.)
D A F♯ G D A
Screamed: Ah! Woo. Ah!
F♯ G D A G
Gtr. 1
Woo. Ah! Woo.
A6sus2
D
Oo, oo, oo, oo, ah, ah, ah, ah. Oo, oo, oo, oo, ah, ah, ah, ah. Oo, oo, oo, oo, ah, ah, ah, ah. Oo, oo, oo, oo, ah, ah, ah, oh.
Gtr. 2
Gtr. 1

Sabertooth Tiger

Words and Music by Brad Shultz, Daniel Tichenor, Jared Champion, Lincoln Parish and Matt Shultz

Copyright © 2010 Sony/ATV Music Publishing LLC, R And R Nomad Music Publishing Co. and 4U2ASKY Entertainment Inc.
All Rights on behalf of Sony/ATV Music Publishing LLC and R And R Nomad Publishing Co.
Administered by Sony/ATV Music Publishing LLC, 8 Music Square West, Nashville, TN 37203
International Copyright Secured All Rights Reserved

Gtr. 2: w/ Rhy. Fig. 1A (last 2 meas., 2 times)
F5 E5 B5 B♭5 A5 F5 E5 B5 B♭5 A5
mouth is full of sand and he's dy - ing to meet _ you. His mouth is full of sand and he's just dy - ing to meet _ you. On the
F5 E5 B5 B♭5 A5 F5 E5 B5 B♭5 A5
oth - er side of town lives a sa - ber - tooth ti - ger. Run a -
Riff B
End Riff B
Gtr. 3
Rhy. Fig. 2
End Rhy. Fig. 2
Gtr. 2
let ring
Chorus
2nd time, Gtr. 4 tacet
Gtr. 3 tacet
A5 G♯5 A5 C5
way, run a - way, run a - way from the beast. Got a bul - let in your back and you're shak - ing at the knees. Run a -
Gtr. 3
Rhy. Fig. 3
End Rhy. Fig. 3
*Gtrs. 1 & 2
*Composite arrangement
To Coda
Gtrs. 1 & 2: w/ Rhy. Fig. 3
A5 G♯5 A5 C5
way, run a - way, run a - way from the beast. Got a bul - let in your back, run a - way from the beast.

*Played behind the beat.

Coda
Interlude
Slower ♩ = 153
Half-time feel
A5 D5 D#5 C5 A5 D5 D#5 G5
Gtr. 5 (slight dist.)
f
w/ bar
A5 D5 D#5 C5 A5 D5 D#5 G5
w/ bar
w/ bar
w/ bar
let ring
+1/2
Gtr. 5 tacet
A5
Screamed:
Ow! Ow! Ow! Ow! Ow! Ow! Ah, na, na, na, na, na, na, na, na, na, na, na, na, na, na, na!
Riff C
End Riff C
Gtrs. 1 & 2
Gtr. 1: w/ Riff C
Ow! Ow! Ow! Ow! Ow! Ow!
Gtr. 2
*fdbk
fdbk.
fdbk.
Pitch: C
C
B♭
*Microphonc fdbk., not caused by string vibration, next 3 meas.

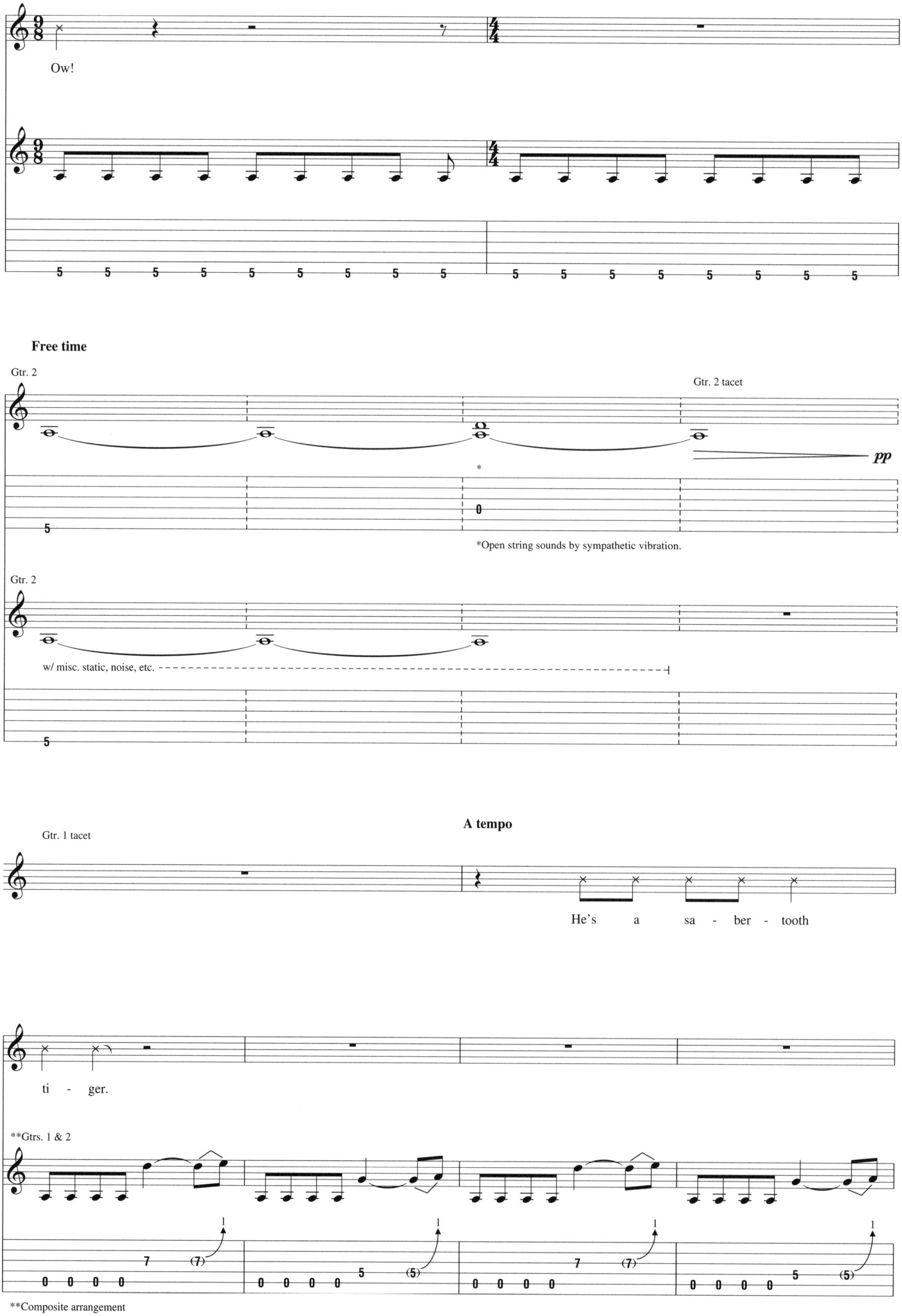
Ow!
Free time
Gtr. 2
Gtr. 2 tacet
pp
*Open string sounds by sympathetic vibration.
Gtr. 2
w/ misc. static, noise, etc.
Gtr. 1 tacet
A tempo
He's a sa - ber - tooth
ti - ger.
**Gtrs. 1 & 2
**Composite arrangement

w/ Lead Voc. ad Lib. (next 8 meas.)
B♭5 A5
Run a -
Outro-Chorus
Gtrs. 1 & 2: w/ Rhy. Fig. 3 (3 1/2 times)
1., 2., 3.
A5 G♯5 A5 C5
way, run a - way, run a - way from the beast. Got a bul - let in your back and you're shak - ing at the knees. Run a -
4.
A5 C5 A5 N.C.
bul - let in your back, run a - way from the beast.
Gtrs. 1 & 2
w/ misc. noise

Japanese Buffalo

Words and Music by Brad Shultz, Daniel Tichenor, Jared Champion, Lincoln Parish and Matt Shultz

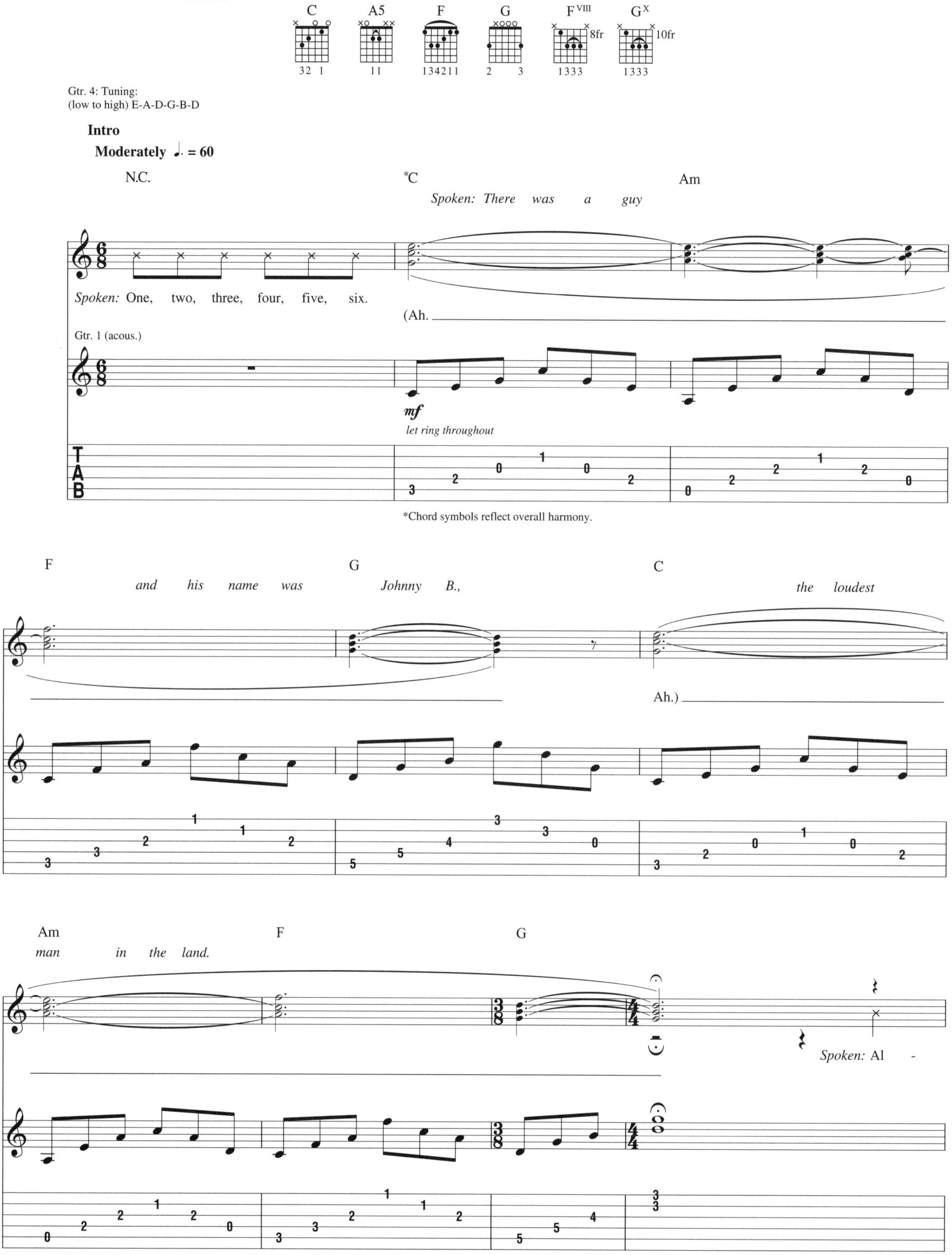

Copyright © 2010 Sony/ATV Music Publishing LLC, R And R Nomad Music Publishing Co. and 4U2ASKY Entertainment Inc.
All Rights on behalf of Sony/ATV Music Publishing LLC and R And R Nomad Publishing Co.
Administered by Sony/ATV Music Publishing LLC, 8 Music Square West, Nashville, TN 37203
International Copyright Secured All Rights Reserved

Faster ♩ = 320
C
A5
C
A5
Rhy. Fig. 1
Gtr. 3 (elec.)
mf
w/ dist.
right. O - kay. Al - right. O - kay. Al -
Gtr. 2 (elec.)
mf
w/ dist.
C
A5
F
End Rhy. Fig. 1
right. O - kay. Uh, huh.
Verse
Gtr. 3: w/ Rhy. Fig. 1 (2 times)
C
A5
C
A5
1. Yelled: How man - y times you cross the line? Run for days with ea - ger eyes.
2. Jap - a - nese from head to toe, and green to red, red to gold.
Riff A

*Composite arrangement **Bass plays F.

C Asus2/F F5 G5
Shame. Oh, oh, oh, oh.
End Rhy. Fig. 2A
End Rhy. Fig. 2
Gtrs. 1 & 3: w/ Rhy. Fig. 2
Gtr. 2: w/ Rhy. Fig. 2A
C Asus2 C Asus2
Screamed: Shame. Shame.
To Coda
End half-time feel
C Asus2 F5 G5
Shame. Oh, oh, oh, oh. Al -
Interlude
Gtr. 2: w/ Riff A
Gtr. 3: w/ Rhy. Fig. 1
C A5 C A5
right. O - kay. Al - right. O - kay. Al -
D.S. al Coda
C A5 F
right. O - kay. Uh, huh.

Coda
F5
G5
rit.
Oh, oh, oh, oh.
Run it o -
Gtr. 3
Gtr. 2
Bridge
Slower ♩. = 66
C
Am7
F
G
- ver my skin like a cheap plas - tic knife. In your
Gtr. 4 (elec.)
mf
w/ dist. & slide
let ring
Riff B
End Riff B
w/ slight dist.
Rhy. Fig. 3
End Rhy. Fig. 3

Gtr. 2: w/ Rhy. Fig. 3 (3 times)
Gtr. 3: w/ Riff B (3 times)
C
Am7
F
G
heart and your mind put me al - ways a - side. Do it
Gtr. 4
let ring
let ring
o - ver a - gain till it cuts to the bone. We can
play by the rules or just leave it a - lone.

Chorus
C5
F7♯11
C5
It's a shame.
It's a
Gtr. 4
steady gliss.
fdbk.
Gtr. 2
8va
loco
fdbk.
1/2
Gtr. 3
w/ dist.
Gtr. 4 tacet
F7♯11
C5
F7♯11
shame.
It's a shame that your
Gtr. 2
1/2
1/2
Gtr. 3

F G F G
heart turned to stone, that your heart turned to stone. Run it
(cont. in slashes)
Bridge
C F G
Rhy. Fig. 4A
End Rhy. Fig. 4A
Gtr. 3
o - ver my skin like a cheap plas - tic knife. In your
Rhy. Fig. 4
End Rhy. Fig. 4
Gtr. 2
Gtrs. 2 & 3: w/ Rhy. Figs. 4 & 4A (3 times)
C F G
heart and your mind put me al - ways a - side. Do it
C F G
o - ver a - gain till it cuts to the bone. We can

C
F
G
play ______ by the rules. It's a shame. It's a shame. It's a
Outro
C
F VIII
G X
Rhy. Fig. 5
End Rhy. Fig. 5
Gtr 3
shame. ______
Gtr. 2
17 17 20 20 13 13 17 12
Gtr. 3: w/ Rhy. Fig. 5
C
F
17 17 20 20 13 13 17
G
E5
N.C.
Gtr. 2
rit.
let ring
12 12 0 12 0
Gtr. 3
rit.
12 12 12 12 10
0 0 X 2 2 0
(2)

Flow

Words and Music by Brad Shultz, Daniel Tichenor, Jared Champion, Lincoln Parish and Matt Shultz

Intro

Moderately ♩ = 107

Gtr. 1: w/ Riff A (2 times)

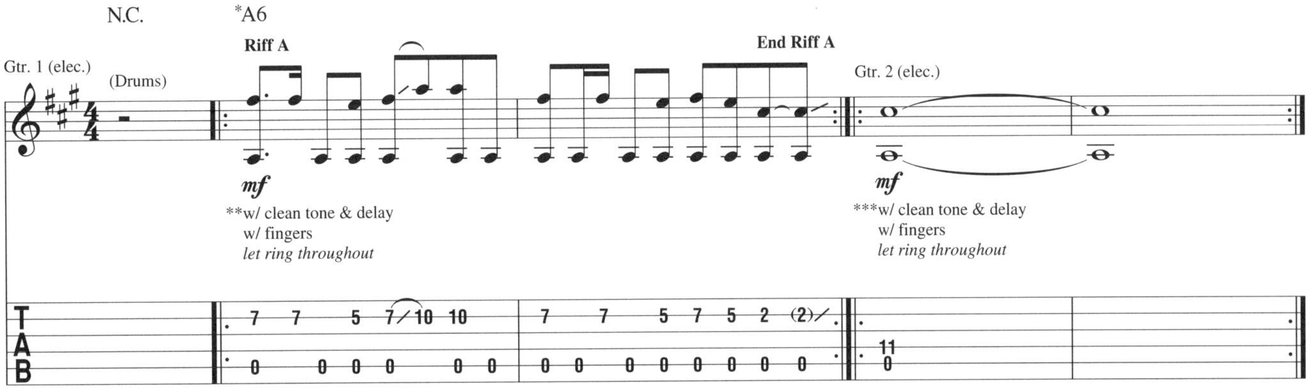

*Chord symbols reflect overall harmony.

**Delay set for sixteenth-note regeneration w/ 1 repeat.

***Delay set for between eighth-note and eighth-note triplet regeneration w/ 3 repeats.

Verse

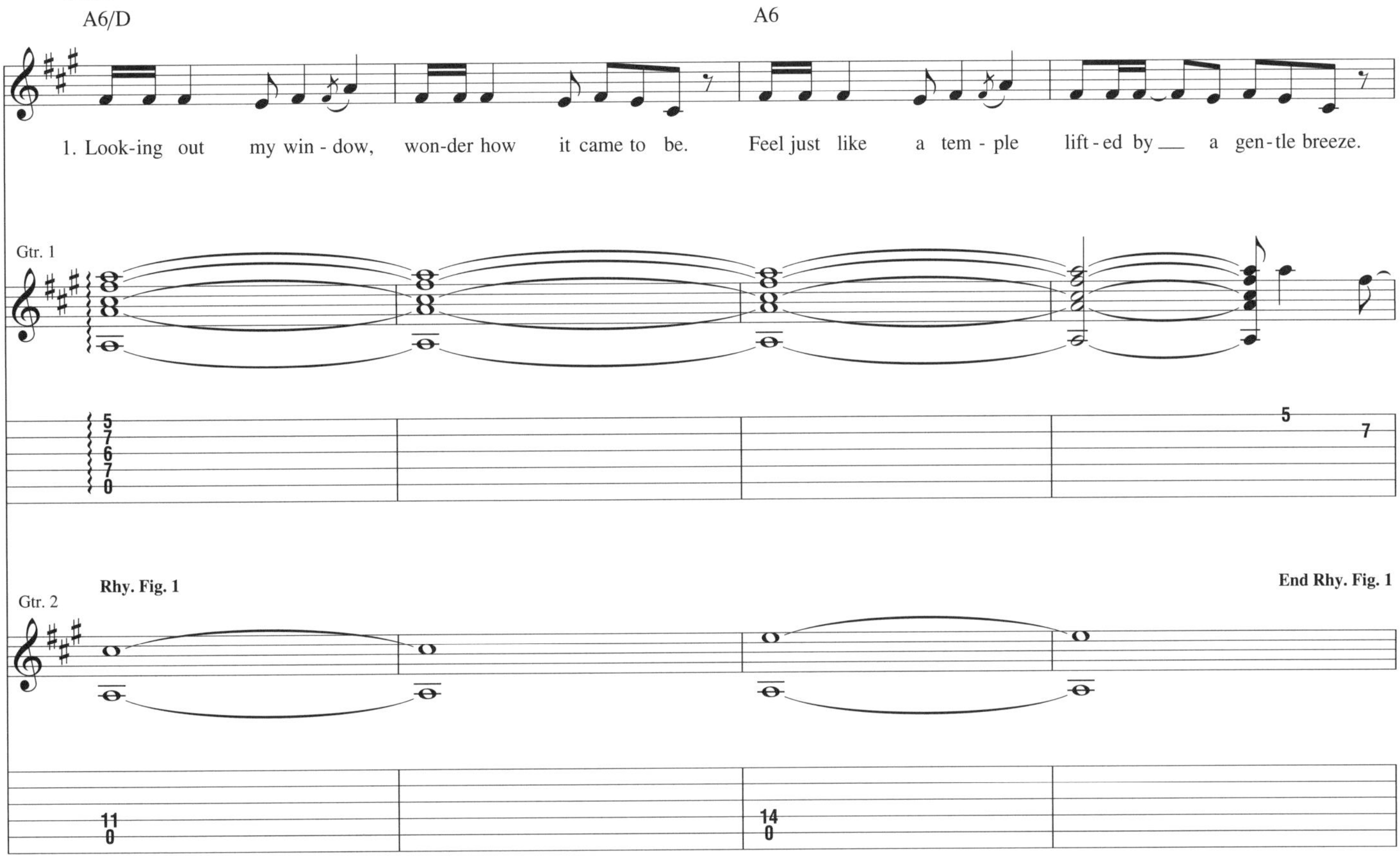

Copyright © 2010 Sony/ATV Music Publishing LLC, R And R Nomad Music Publishing Co. and 4U2ASKY Entertainment Inc.
All Rights on behalf of Sony/ATV Music Publishing LLC and R And R Nomad Publishing Co.
Administered by Sony/ATV Music Publishing LLC, 8 Music Square West, Nashville, TN 37203
International Copyright Secured All Rights Reserved

Gtr. 2: w/ Rhy. Fig. 1
A6/D
A6
Ug - ly as a suit - case, I can see it stretch for days. Hang - ing on a sun - set, soft - ly tram - pled by the rain.
Gtr. 1
Chorus
A6/D
A6
Way too long, hold on, hold on. Dead and gone,
Gtr. 1
Gtr. 2
A6/D
so long, hold on. Way too long, hold on, hold on.

To Coda
A6
Dead and gone,
so long, hold on,
so long, hold on.
Interlude
A6/D
Riff B
A6
End Riff B
Gtr. 1
Gtr. 2
Riff B1
Gtr. 3 (acous.)
End Riff B1
mf
w/ fingers
let ring throughout

Verse
D.S. al Coda
Gtr. 2: w/ Rhy. Fig. 1
Gtr. 3 tacet
A6/D
A6
2. Look-ing out my win - dow, try-ing to find a hid-ing place. Climb in-to the tree - tops, watch it all just drift a-way.
Gtr. 1
Coda
Interlude
w/ bkgd. yelling (next 12 meas.)
Gtrs. 1 & 3: w/ Riffs B & B1
A6/D
A6
Gtr. 2
A6/D
A6
Riff C
End Riff C
Gtr. 1
Riff C1
End Riff C1
Gtr. 3
Gtr. 2

Gtrs. 1 & 3: w/ Riffs C & C1
A6/D
A6
Gtr. 2
Chorus
A6/D
Gtrs. 1 & 2 tacet
A6
Way too long, hold on, hold on. Dead and gone,
Gtr. 1
Gtr. 3
Gtr. 2
Rhy. Fill 1
End Rhy. Fill 1
A6/D
so long, hold on. Way too long, hold on, hold on.
Gtr. 3

Outro
A6
A6/D
Dead and gone, so long, hold on, hold on, hold on, hold on, hold on,
Gtr. 1
Riff D
Gtr. 3
A6
A6/D
hold on, hold on, hold on, hold on, hold on, hold on,

A6
hold on, hold on, hold on, hold on, hold on, hold on.
End Riff D
Gtr. 1: w/ Riff D
A6/D
Spoken: You can just mix that down with-out me.
Gtr. 3
A6
A6/D

A6
Gtr. 3: w/ Rhy. Fill 1 (2 times)
A6/D
A
A/G
Gtr. 1
Asus2
A/G
A5
Gtr. 3
Gtr. 1
Harm.

Shiver

Words and Music by Brad Shultz, Daniel Tichenor, Jared Champion, Lincoln Parish and Matt Shultz

Copyright © 2010 Sony/ATV Music Publishing LLC, R And R Nomad Music Publishing Co. and 4U2ASKY Entertainment Inc.
All Rights on behalf of Sony/ATV Music Publishing LLC and R And R Nomad Publishing Co.
Administered by Sony/ATV Music Publishing LLC, 8 Music Square West, Nashville, TN 37203
International Copyright Secured All Rights Reserved

Verse
Gtr. 1: w/ Rhy. Fig. 1 (2 times)
C
Gtr. 2 tacet
Em
1. Tim - ber shakes these trails. They all de - rail,
pho - ny, false and frail.
Am
G
An emp - ty o - cean, lost our way with no di - rec - tion home.
C
Em
Gold - en nee - dles, names we take in vain.
Find it hard - er to re - main.
Am
G
G
Rhy. Fill 1
End Rhy. Fill 1
Gtr. 1
No, noth - ing sa - cred. Still wait - ing on that ex - plain - a - tion.
Chorus
C
Rhy. Fig. 2
G5
Right be - fore my eyes I saw the whole world lose con - trol. The whole
Gtr. 2

Am F G5
End Rhy. Fig. 2
world lost con - trol be - fore my eyes, uh, huh.
Gtr. 1: w/ Rhy. Fig. 2
C G5
I fell through the floor, I could - n't take it an - y - more. I can't
Am F G5
take this an - y - more, it breaks my mind, uh, huh.
Verse
Gtr. 1: w/ Rhy. Fig. 1 (2 times)
C Em
2. Hold her dirt - y hands o - ver the flames, get - ting pleas - ure from the pain.
let ring

Am
G
Soft-ly scream-ing, the pis-tol that you raise has spo-ken.
C
Em
Gold-en nee-dles, names we take in vain.
Find it hard-er to re-main.
let ring
Gtr. 1: w/ Rhy. Fill 1
Am
G
No, noth-ing sa-cred. Still wait-ing on that ex-plain-a-tion.
let ring
Chorus
Gtr. 1: w/ Rhy. Fig. 2 (2 times)
C
G
Right be-fore my eyes I saw the whole world lose con-trol. The whole
let ring

Am F G
world lost con - trol before my eyes, uh, huh.
Rhy. Fig. 3
End Rhy. Fig. 3
C G
I fell through the floor, I could-n't take it an - y - more. I can't
Gtr. 2: w/ Rhy. Fig. 3
Am F G
take this an - y - more, it breaks my mind, uh, huh.
Bridge
F Am
Rhy. Fig. 4
End Rhy. Fig. 4
Gtr. 1
Ev - 'ry - thing I thought I knew fell to the side.
Gtr. 2

Gtr. 1: w/ Rhy. Fig. 4
F
Am
Time went on and on, I could-n't see past my own eyes, past my
G5
Gtr. 1
Am
eyes, past my eyes,
*Played ahead of the beat.
G
(cont. in notation)
past my eyes.

Outro-Chorus

GUITAR NOTATION LEGEND

Guitar music can be notated three different ways: on a *musical staff*, in *tablature*, and in *rhythm slashes*.

RHYTHM SLASHES are written above the staff. Strum chords in the rhythm indicated. Use the chord diagrams found at the top of the first page of the transcription for the appropriate chord voicings. Round noteheads indicate single notes.

THE MUSICAL STAFF shows pitches and rhythms and is divided by bar lines into measures. Pitches are named after the first seven letters of the alphabet.

TABLATURE graphically represents the guitar fingerboard. Each horizontal line represents a string, and each number represents a fret.

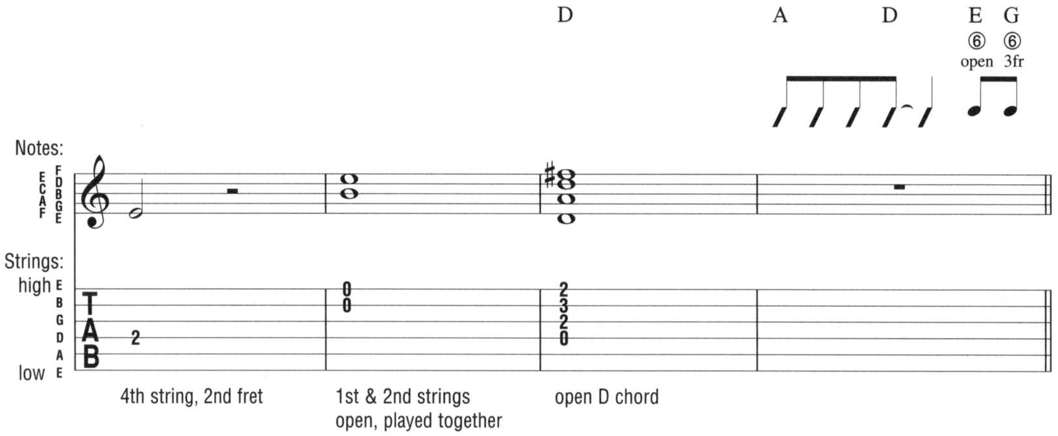

Definitions for Special Guitar Notation

HALF-STEP BEND: Strike the note and bend up 1/2 step.

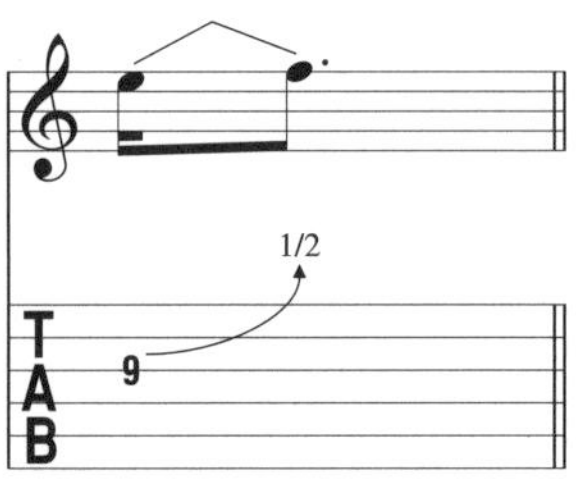

WHOLE-STEP BEND: Strike the note and bend up one step.

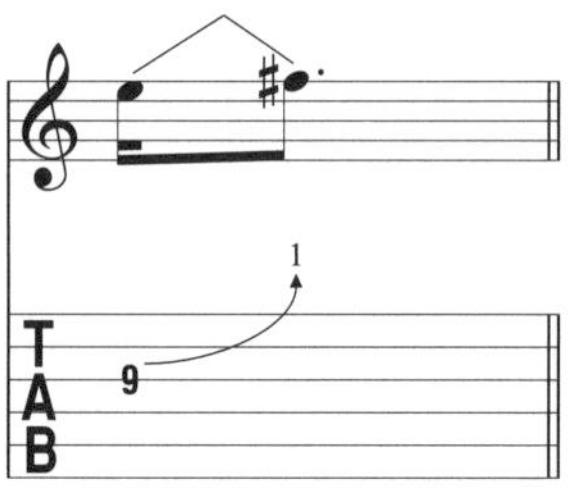

GRACE NOTE BEND: Strike the note and immediately bend up as indicated.

SLIGHT (MICROTONE) BEND: Strike the note and bend up 1/4 step.

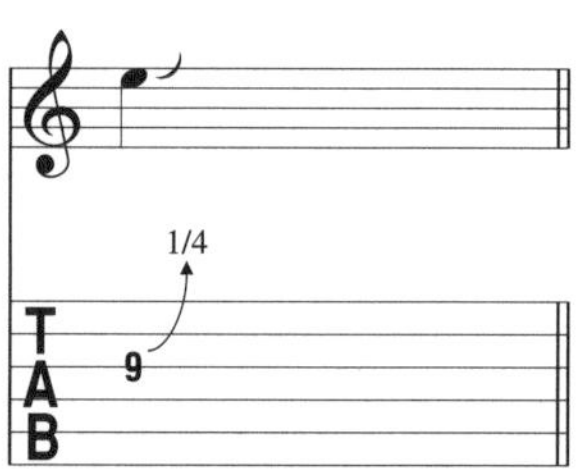

BEND AND RELEASE: Strike the note and bend up as indicated, then release back to the original note. Only the first note is struck.

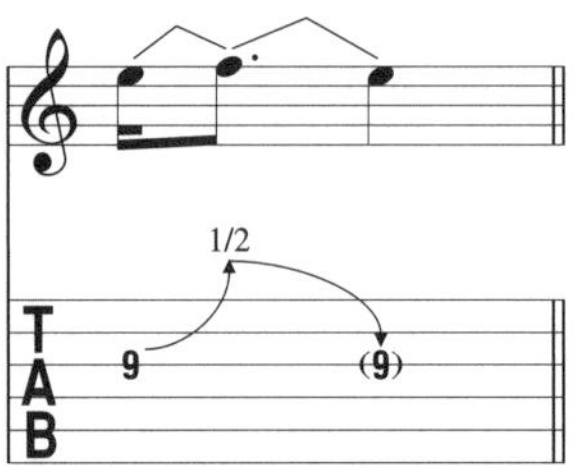

PRE-BEND: Bend the note as indicated, then strike it.

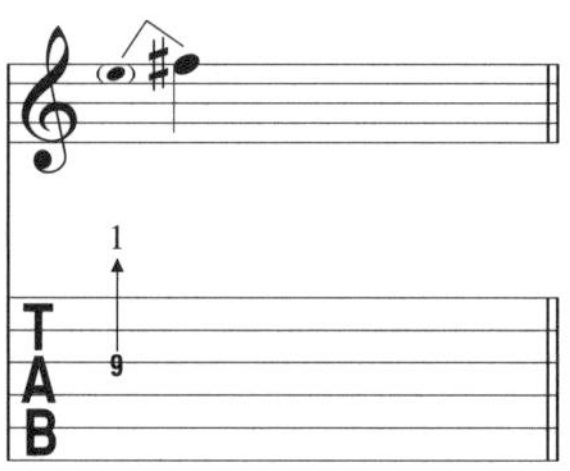

PRE-BEND AND RELEASE: Bend the note as indicated. Strike it and release the bend back to the original note.

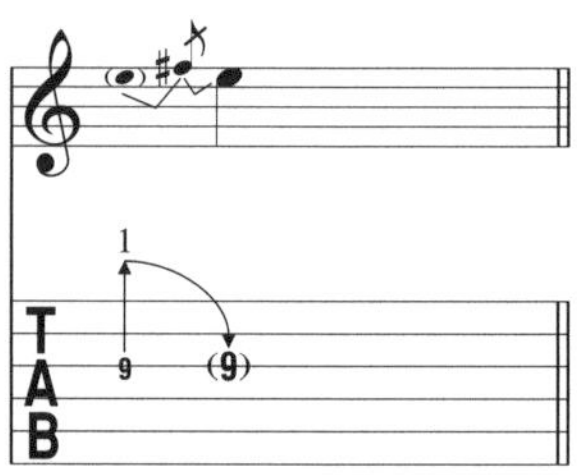

UNISON BEND: Strike the two notes simultaneously and bend the lower note up to the pitch of the higher.

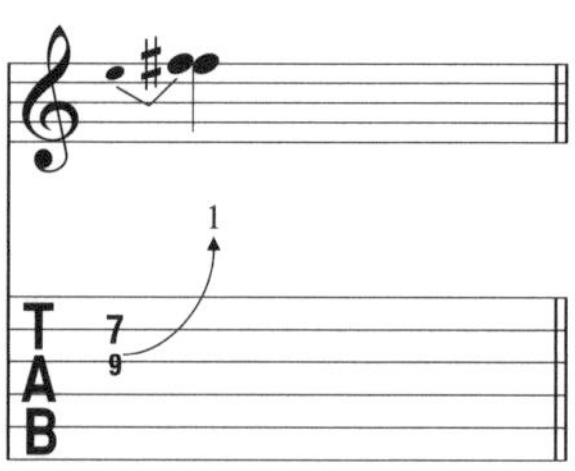

VIBRATO: The string is vibrated by rapidly bending and releasing the note with the fretting hand.

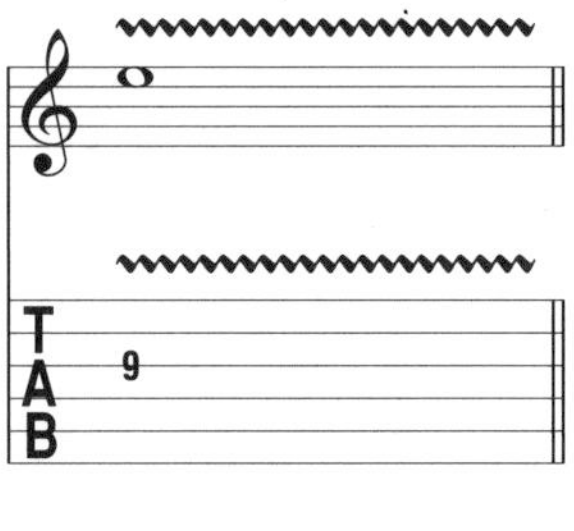

WIDE VIBRATO: The pitch is varied to a greater degree by vibrating with the fretting hand.

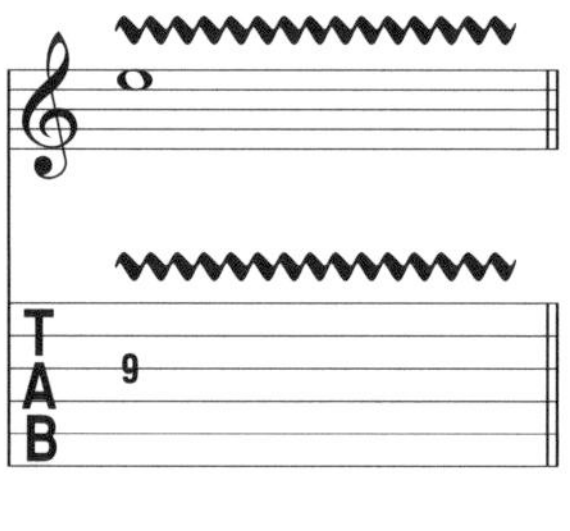

HAMMER-ON: Strike the first (lower) note with one finger, then sound the higher note (on the same string) with another finger by fretting it without picking.

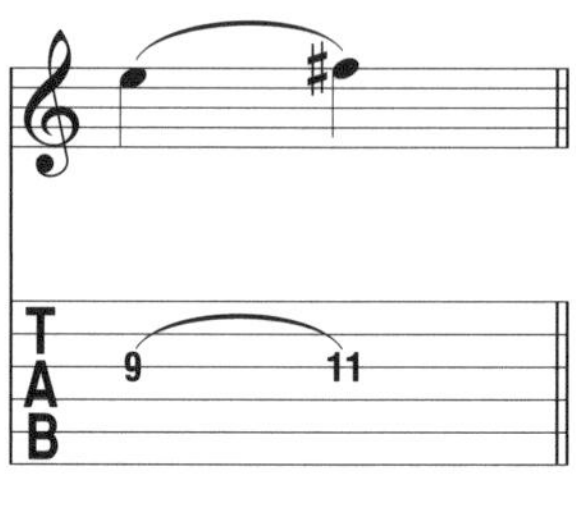

PULL-OFF: Place both fingers on the notes to be sounded. Strike the first note and without picking, pull the finger off to sound the second (lower) note.

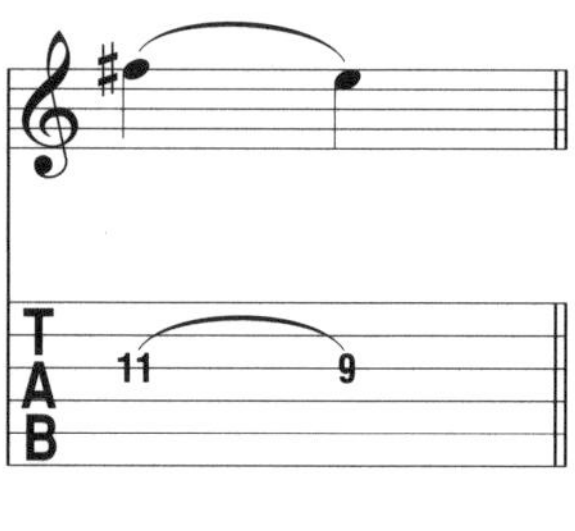

LEGATO SLIDE: Strike the first note and then slide the same fret-hand finger up or down to the second note. The second note is not struck.

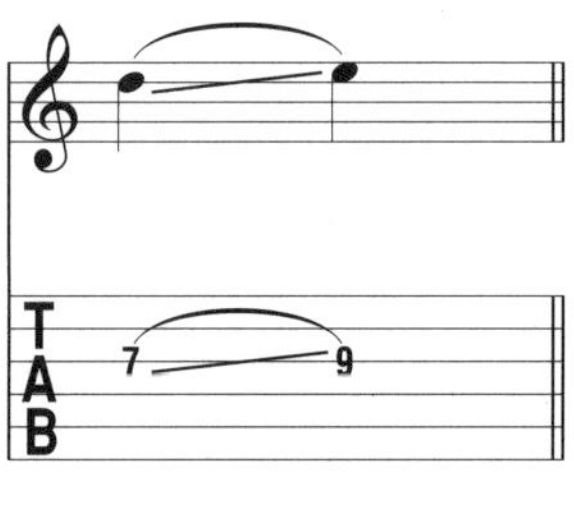

SHIFT SLIDE: Same as legato slide, except the second note is struck.

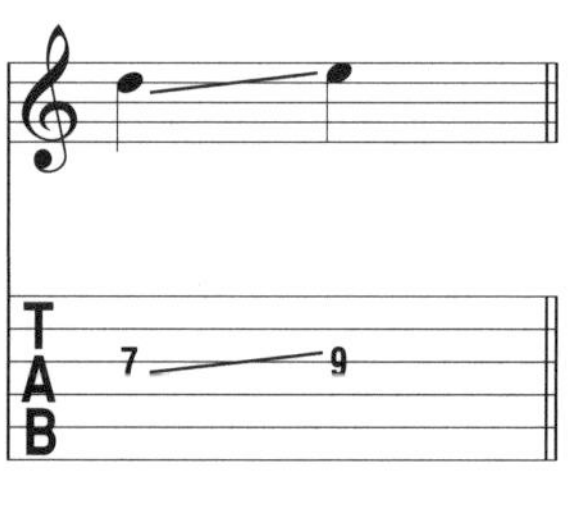

TRILL: Very rapidly alternate between the notes indicated by continuously hammering on and pulling off.

TAPPING: Hammer ("tap") the fret indicated with the pick-hand index or middle finger and pull off to the note fretted by the fret hand.

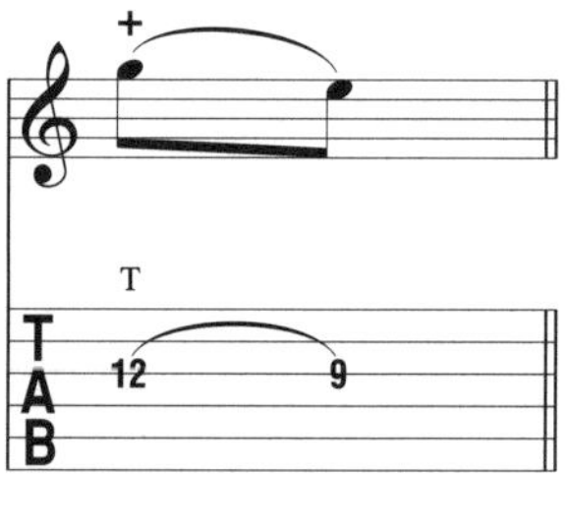

NATURAL HARMONIC: Strike the note while the fret-hand lightly touches the string directly over the fret indicated.

PINCH HARMONIC: The note is fretted normally and a harmonic is produced by adding the edge of the thumb or the tip of the index finger of the pick hand to the normal pick attack.

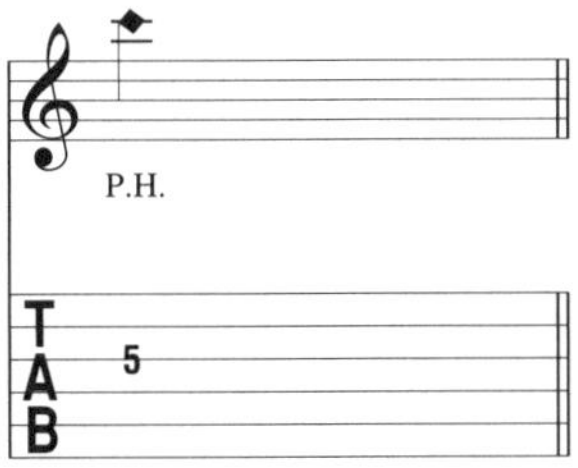

HARP HARMONIC: The note is fretted normally and a harmonic is produced by gently resting the pick hand's index finger directly above the indicated fret (in parentheses) while the pick hand's thumb or pick assists by plucking the appropriate string.

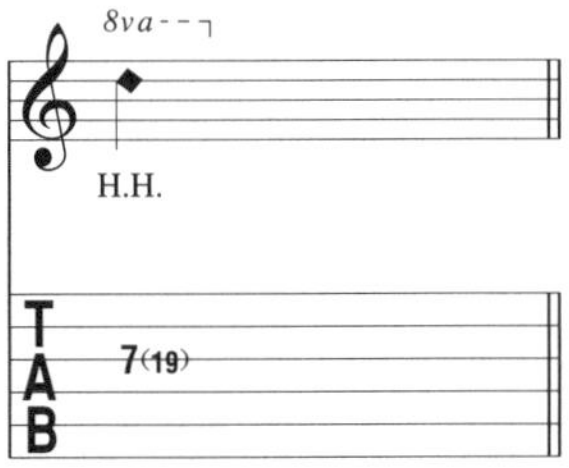

PICK SCRAPE: The edge of the pick is rubbed down (or up) the string, producing a scratchy sound.

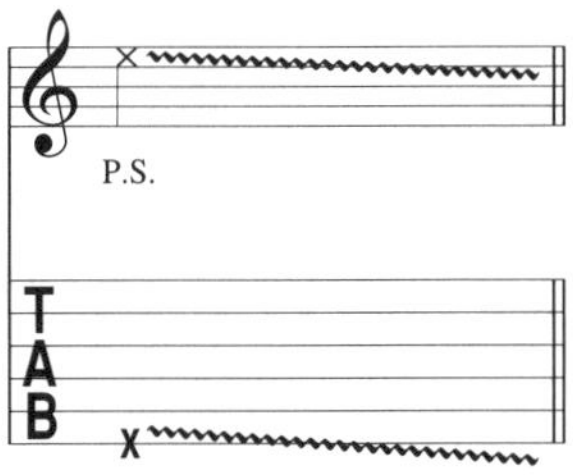

MUFFLED STRINGS: A percussive sound is produced by laying the fret hand across the string(s) without depressing, and striking them with the pick hand.

PALM MUTING: The note is partially muted by the pick hand lightly touching the string(s) just before the bridge.

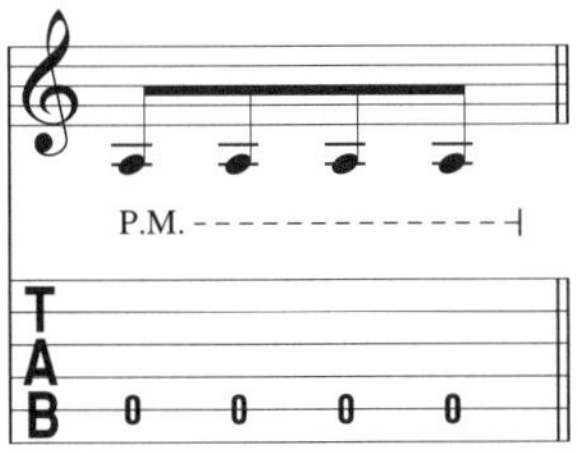

RAKE: Drag the pick across the strings indicated with a single motion.

TREMOLO PICKING: The note is picked as rapidly and continuously as possible.

ARPEGGIATE: Play the notes of the chord indicated by quickly rolling them from bottom to top.

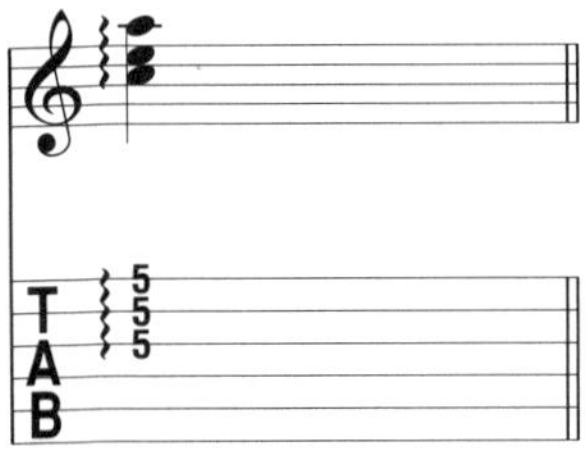

VIBRATO BAR DIVE AND RETURN: The pitch of the note or chord is dropped a specified number of steps (in rhythm), then returned to the original pitch.

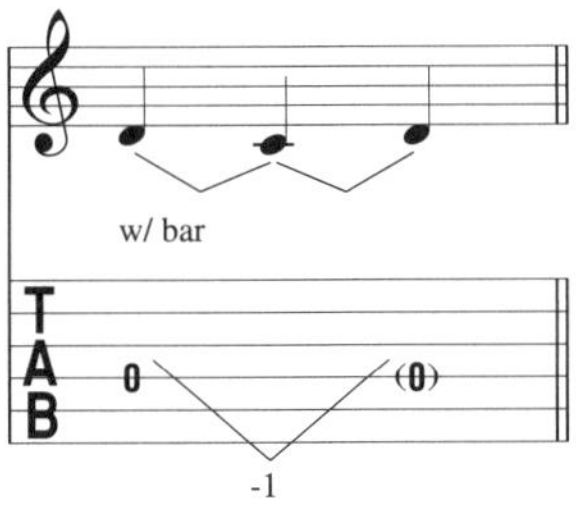

VIBRATO BAR SCOOP: Depress the bar just before striking the note, then quickly release the bar.

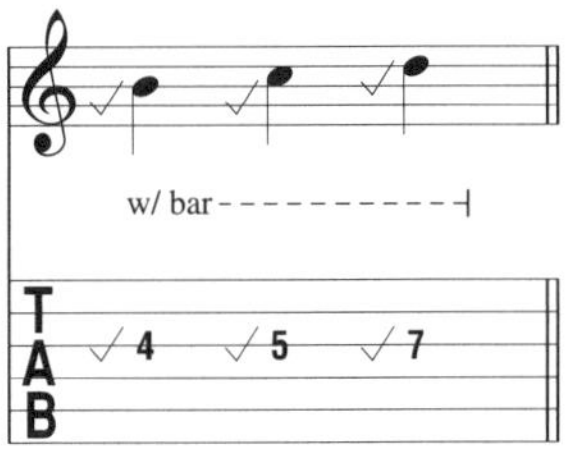

VIBRATO BAR DIP: Strike the note and then immediately drop a specified number of steps, then release back to the original pitch.

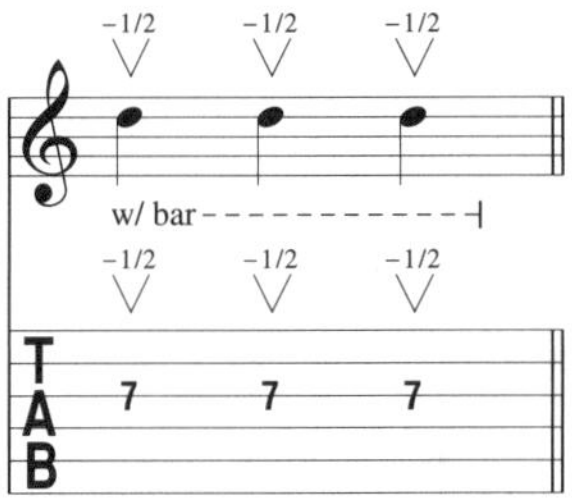

Additional Musical Definitions

(accent) • Accentuate note (play it louder).

(accent) • Accentuate note with great intensity.

(staccato) • Play the note short.

⊓ • Downstroke

V • Upstroke

D.S. al Coda • Go back to the sign (𝄋), then play until the measure marked "***To Coda***," then skip to the section labelled "**Coda**."

D.C. al Fine • Go back to the beginning of the song and play until the measure marked "***Fine***" (end).

Rhy. Fig. • Label used to recall a recurring accompaniment pattern (usually chordal).

Riff • Label used to recall composed, melodic lines (usually single notes) which recur.

Fill • Label used to identify a brief melodic figure which is to be inserted into the arrangement.

Rhy. Fill • A chordal version of a Fill.

tacet • Instrument is silent (drops out).

• Repeat measures between signs.

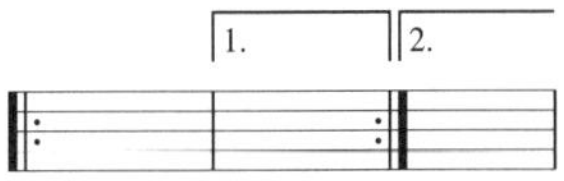

• When a repeated section has different endings, play the first ending only the first time and the second ending only the second time.

NOTE: Tablature numbers in parentheses mean:
1. The note is being sustained over a system (note in standard notation is tied), or
2. The note is sustained, but a new articulation (such as a hammer-on, pull-off, slide or vibrato) begins, or
3. The note is a barely audible "ghost" note (note in standard notation is also in parentheses).

RECORDED VERSIONS®

The Best Note-For-Note Transcriptions Available

ALL BOOKS INCLUDE TABLATURE

14037551 AC/DC – Backtracks $32.99
00692015 Aerosmith – Greatest Hits $22.95
00690178 Alice in Chains – Acoustic $19.95
00694865 Alice in Chains – Dirt $19.95
00690812 All American Rejects – Move Along $19.95
00690958 Duane Allman Guitar Anthology $24.99
00694932 Allman Brothers Band – Volume 1 .... $24.95
00694933 Allman Brothers Band – Volume 2 .... $24.95
00694934 Allman Brothers Band – Volume 3 .... $24.95
00690865 Atreyu – A Deathgrip on Yesterday $19.95
00690609 Audioslave $19.95
00690820 Avenged Sevenfold – City of Evil $24.95
00690366 Bad Company – Original Anthology $19.95
00690503 Beach Boys – Very Best of $19.95
00690489 Beatles – 1 .... $24.99
00694832 Beatles – For Acoustic Guitar $22.99
00691014 Beatles Rock Band $34.99
00690110 Beatles – White Album (Book 1) $19.95
00691043 Jeff Beck – Wired $19.99
00692385 Chuck Berry $19.95
00690835 Billy Talent $19.95
00690901 Best of Black Sabbath $19.95
00690831 blink-182 – Greatest Hits $19.95
00690913 Boston $19.95
00690932 Boston – Don't Look Back $19.99
00690491 David Bowie – Best of $19.95
00690873 Breaking Benjamin – Phobia $19.95
00690451 Jeff Buckley – Collection $24.95
00690957 Bullet for My Valentine – Scream Aim Fire ... $19.95
00691004 Chickenfoot $22.99
00690590 Eric Clapton – Anthology $29.95
00690415 Clapton Chronicles – Best of Eric Clapton $18.95
00690936 Eric Clapton – Complete Clapton $29.99
00690074 Eric Clapton – The Cream of Clapton $24.95
00694869 Eric Clapton – Unplugged $22.95
00690162 The Clash – Best of $19.95
00690828 Coheed & Cambria – Good Apollo I'm Burning Star, IV, Vol. 1: From Fear Through the Eyes of Madness $19.95
00690593 Coldplay – A Rush of Blood to the Head $19.95
00690962 Coldplay – Viva La Vida $19.95
00690819 Creedence Clearwater Revival – Best of $22.95
00690648 The Very Best of Jim Croce $19.95
00690613 Crosby, Stills & Nash – Best of $22.95
00690967 Death Cab for Cutie – Narrow Stairs $22.99
00690289 Deep Purple – Best of $17.95
00690784 Def Leppard – Best of $19.95
00692240 Bo Diddley $19.99
00690347 The Doors – Anthology $22.95
00690348 The Doors – Essential Guitar Collection $16.95
00690810 Fall Out Boy – From Under the Cork Tree $19.95
00690664 Fleetwood Mac – Best of $19.95
00690870 Flyleaf $19.95
00690931 Foo Fighters – Echoes, Silence, Patience & Grace $19.95
00690808 Foo Fighters – In Your Honor $19.95
00690805 Robben Ford – Best of $19.95
00694920 Free – Best of $19.95
00691050 Glee Guitar Collection $19.99
00690848 Godsmack – IV $19.95
00690943 The Goo Goo Dolls – Greatest Hits Volume 1: The Singles $22.95
00701764 Guitar Tab White Pages – Play-Along $39.99
00694854 Buddy Guy – Damn Right, I've Got the Blues $19.95
00690840 Ben Harper – Both Sides of the Gun $19.95
00694798 George Harrison – Anthology $19.95
00690841 Scott Henderson – Blues Guitar Collection .. $19.95
00692930 Jimi Hendrix – Are You Experienced? $24.95
00692931 Jimi Hendrix – Axis: Bold As Love $22.95
00692932 Jimi Hendrix – Electric Ladyland $24.95
00690017 Jimi Hendrix – Live at Woodstock $24.95
00690602 Jimi Hendrix – Smash Hits $24.99
00690793 John Lee Hooker Anthology $24.99
00690692 Billy Idol – Very Best of $19.95
00690688 Incubus – A Crow Left of the Murder $19.95
00690544 Incubus – Morningview $19.95
00690790 Iron Maiden Anthology $24.99
00690721 Jet – Get Born $19.95
00690684 Jethro Tull – Aqualung $19.95
00690959 John5 – Requiem $22.95
00690814 John5 – Songs for Sanity $19.95
00690751 John5 – Vertigo $19.95
00690845 Eric Johnson – Bloom $19.95
00690846 Jack Johnson and Friends – Sing-A-Longs and Lullabies for the Film Curious George $19.95
00690271 Robert Johnson – New Transcriptions $24.95
00699131 Janis Joplin – Best of $19.95
00690427 Judas Priest – Best of $22.99
00690742 The Killers – Hot Fuss $19.95
00690975 Kings of Leon – Only by the Night $22.99
00694903 Kiss – Best of $24.95
00690355 Kiss – Destroyer $16.95
00690834 Lamb of God – Ashes of the Wake $19.95
00690875 Lamb of God – Sacrament $19.95
00690823 Ray LaMontagne – Trouble $19.95
00690679 John Lennon – Guitar Collection $19.95
00690781 Linkin Park – Hybrid Theory $22.95
00690743 Los Lonely Boys $19.95
00690720 Lostprophets – Start Something $19.95
00690955 Lynyrd Skynyrd – All-Time Greatest Hits $19.99
00694954 Lynyrd Skynyrd – New Best of $19.95
00690754 Marilyn Manson – Lest We Forget $19.95
00694956 Bob Marley– Legend $19.95
00694945 Bob Marley– Songs of Freedom $24.95
00690657 Maroon5 – Songs About Jane $19.95
00120080 Don McLean – Songbook $19.95
00694951 Megadeth – Rust in Peace $22.95
00690951 Megadeth – United Abominations $22.99
00690505 John Mellencamp – Guitar Collection $19.95
00690646 Pat Metheny – One Quiet Night $19.95
00690558 Pat Metheny – Trio: 99>00 .... $19.95
00690040 Steve Miller Band – Young Hearts $19.95
00694883 Nirvana – Nevermind $19.95
00690026 Nirvana – Unplugged in New York $19.95
00690807 The Offspring – Greatest Hits $19.95
00694847 Ozzy Osbourne – Best of $22.95
00690399 Ozzy Osbourne – Ozzman Cometh $22.99
00690933 Best of Brad Paisley $22.95
00690995 Brad Paisley – Play: The Guitar Album $24.99
00690866 Panic! At the Disco – A Fever You Can't Sweat Out $19.95
00690938 Christopher Parkening – Duets & Concertos $24.99
00694855 Pearl Jam – Ten $19.95
00690439 A Perfect Circle – Mer De Noms $19.95
00690499 Tom Petty – Definitive Guitar Collection $19.95
00690428 Pink Floyd – Dark Side of the Moon $19.95
00690789 Poison – Best of $19.95
00693864 The Police – Best of $19.95
00694975 Queen – Greatest Hits $24.95
00690670 Queensryche – Very Best of $19.95
00690878 The Raconteurs – Broken Boy Soldiers $19.95
00694910 Rage Against the Machine $19.95
00690055 Red Hot Chili Peppers – Blood Sugar Sex Magik $19.95
00690584 Red Hot Chili Peppers – By the Way $19.95
00690852 Red Hot Chili Peppers –Stadium Arcadium .. $24.95
00690511 Django Reinhardt – Definitive Collection $19.95
00690779 Relient K – MMHMM $19.95
00690631 Rolling Stones – Guitar Anthology $27.95
00694976 Rolling Stones – Some Girls $22.95
00690264 The Rolling Stones – Tattoo You $19.95
00690685 David Lee Roth – Eat 'Em and Smile $19.95
00690942 David Lee Roth and the Songs of Van Halen . $19.95
00690031 Santana's Greatest Hits $19.95
00690566 Scorpions – Best of $22.95
00690604 Bob Seger – Guitar Collection $19.95
00690803 Kenny Wayne Shepherd Band – Best of $19.95
00690968 Shinedown – The Sound of Madness $22.99
00690813 Slayer – Guitar Collection $19.95
00690733 Slipknot – Vol. 3 (The Subliminal Verses) $22.99
00120004 Steely Dan – Best of $24.95
00694921 Steppenwolf – Best of $22.95
00690655 Mike Stern – Best of $19.95
00690877 Stone Sour – Come What(ever) May $19.95
00690520 Styx Guitar Collection $19.95
00120081 Sublime $19.95
00120122 Sublime – 40oz. to Freedom $19.95
00690929 Sum 41 – Underclass Hero $19.95
00690767 Switchfoot – The Beautiful Letdown $19.95
00690993 Taylor Swift – Fearless $22.99
00690830 System of a Down – Hypnotize $19.95
00690799 System of a Down – Mezmerize $19.95
00690531 System of a Down – Toxicity $19.95
00694824 James Taylor – Best of $16.95
00690871 Three Days Grace – One-X $19.95
00690737 3 Doors Down – The Better Life $22.95
00690683 Robin Trower – Bridge of Sighs $19.95
00699191 U2 – Best of: 1980-1990 .... $19.95
00690732 U2 – Best of: 1990-2000 .... $19.95
00660137 Steve Vai – Passion & Warfare $24.95
00690116 Stevie Ray Vaughan – Guitar Collection $24.95
00660058 Stevie Ray Vaughan – Lightnin' Blues 1983-1987 .... $24.95
00694835 Stevie Ray Vaughan – The Sky Is Crying $22.95
00690015 Stevie Ray Vaughan – Texas Flood $19.95
00690772 Velvet Revolver – Contraband $22.95
00690071 Weezer (The Blue Album) $19.95
00690966 Weezer – (Red Album) $19.99
00690447 The Who – Best of $24.95
00690916 The Best of Dwight Yoakam $19.95
00690905 Neil Young – Rust Never Sleeps $19.99
00690623 Frank Zappa – Over-Nite Sensation $22.99
00690589 ZZ Top Guitar Anthology $24.95

Prices and availability subject to change without notice. Some products may not be available outside the U.S.A.

FOR A COMPLETE LIST OF GUITAR RECORDED VERSIONS TITLES, SEE YOUR LOCAL MUSIC DEALER, OR WRITE TO:

HAL•LEONARD® CORPORATION

7777 W. BLUEMOUND RD. P.O. BOX 13819 MILWAUKEE, WI 53213

Visit Hal Leonard online at www.halleonard.com

0211